The Let's Series of ESL

LET'S BEGIN

D0113200

The Let's Series of ESL

Phase O+: Let's Begin
Phase 1: Let's Converse
Phase 2: Let's Read
Phase 3: Let's Write
Phase 4: Let's Continue

The Let's Series of ESL

LET'S BEGIN

Phase Zero Plus

William Samelson

PE1128.S2174 2007
vol. 1 (phase 0+)
Samelson, William, 1928–
author.
English as a second language
Baltimore [Maryland] :
Elstreet Educational,

ELSTREET
EDUCATIONAL
Baltimore • Washington

Cover Illustrations by Edward Molina
Cover Design by Ross Feldner

EDUCATIONAL

PO Box 858
Savage, MD 20763
800-296-1961
www.Elstreet.com

Library of Congress Cataloging-in-Publication Data

Samelson, William, 1928-
  English as a second language : phase zero plus, let's begin / William
Samelson. —2nd ed.
      p. cm.
  Includes index.
  ISBN 978-0-935437-30-0 (pbk.)
  1. English language—Textbooks for foreign speakers. 2. Sec-
ond language acquisition—Problems, exercises, etc. 3. English lan-
guage—Grammar—Problems, exercises, etc. I. Title.
  PE1128.S2174 2007
  428.2'4--dc22

                                2007034801

Printed in the United States of America

To my youngest daughter Karin, with love

Contents

Preface   xi

Acknowledgements   xv

Getting Started   1
Penmanship
The Alphabet: Spelling, Writing
Syllabification
Important Sound

Chapter One   **Hello and Goodbye**   15
Questions with *wh* and *is / how* and *where*
Present Time of the verbs *to have* and *to be*
Contractions: *we've / you've / they've / what's / it's* etc.
Affirmative statement: Noun Phrase + Verb Phrase
Demonstratives: *this / that*
Singular and Plural

Chapter Two   **Meet My Friends**   37
Negatives: *no / not*
Personal Pronouns: *I / you / he / she / it / we / you / they*
Demonstrative Pronoun Subjects: *this / that / here / there*
Questions with *what*
Negative Contractions: *isn't / aren't*
Nationalities

Chapter Three **See You At 7 O'Clock** 59

Grammatical Summary

Possessive Adjectives: *my / your / his / her / our / their*

Present Continuous of Verbs: *be + Verb + ing*

Numbers 0 (zero) to 20 (twenty)

Telling Time: *when? / early / late / on time / always / never / today / o'clock*

Chapter Four **Dinner at the Carsons** 85

Possessive Pronouns: Question *whose? Mine / yours / his / hers / ours / yours / theirs*

Predispositions: *in / at / on / behind / to / by / under / inside*

Days of the Week: *Monday / Tuesday / Wednesday / Thursday / Friday / Saturday / Sunday*

One and Many - Singular and Plural

Ordinal Numbers: *First / Second / Third / etc.*

Chapter Five **A Trip to the Zoo** 113

Command and Polite Request: *would you...? / shall we...? / let's...*

Demonstratives: *these / those*

Adjectives = Words that Describe

Use of *where / tag question*

The Seasons: *Spring / Summer / Fall / Winter*

Months: *January / February / March / April / May / June / July / August / September / October / November / December*

Object Pronouns

Chapter Six **It Surely is Cold Today** 149

Use of *and / but / or*

The Weather: *cold / warm / mild / it rains/ it snows / it's windy / it's hot*

Direction: *North / South / East / West*
Continuation of Adjectives / Descriptive Words
Compound Sentences
The Human Body

Chapter Seven   **At the Supermarket**   175
Use of *and / too*
Colors: *brown / red/ white / black / yellow / blue /*
    orange / green / grey
Use of *everybody / nobody*
Use of *as...as*
Use of *around / in / on / to / with*

Chapter Eight   **Our Family**   207
Object Pronouns (review)
Direct and Indirect Object Nouns and Pronouns
Comparatives of Adjectives and Adverbs
Use of *more / bigger/ better / than*
Use of *too + Adverb*

Chapter Nine   **Our Home**   233
Review and Use of *Wh-* Questions
Positions: *above/ below / under / on top of /*
    in front of / next to / beside / behind
Use of *a / an / the / some*
Comparison of Adjective and Adverbs

Chapter Ten   **Our Town**   261
Directions: *right / left / straight ahead / around the*
    corner / opposite / follow / block / across
Review the Use of *in / on / at* with *time and place*
Adjectives and Adverbs Comparisons
Use of *alike / different / the same / similar*
Use of *turn on / turn off*

Appendix A   Active Vocabulary   289

Appendix B   Contractions Appearing in this Book 295

Appendix C   Some Irregular Verbs   296

Appendix D   Some Regular Adjective and Adverbs 297

Appendix E   Some Irregular Comparative Forms of Some
                Adjectives and Adverbs 298

                Index   299

Preface

Phase Zero Plus: Let's Begin is the first level in learning English as a second language. Let's Begin is designed either for classroom use or for individual study with or without an instructor. The book is intended for students on the elementary level of their study of English, regardless of age. It is aimed at students who are natives of foreign countries wishing to acquire a basic level of English proficiency in an English-speaking environment.

The aim of Let's Begin is to enable non-English-speaking students to understand speakers of English and to communicate their basic needs to them. To this end, the exercises and practice sections are presented to provide learning experiences in listening, talking, reading, and writing. The exercises are varied, and their scope is geared toward grammar-based activities. In the more advanced texts of this series, Phases I, II, III, and IV, emphasis is placed on contextualization and function-based exercises.

It is hoped that Let's Begin will enable students of English as a Second Language to enjoy their study experience. The concern here is to provide a challenging text so that teacher and student alike may become involved in a productive and rewarding process of guiding and learning, respectively. The end result of this process will, hopefully, yield communicative confidence in all four areas: listening, speaking, reading, and writing on a basic level.

The text does not presuppose any knowledge of basic grammar and verb usage. All chapters allow for the teaching of certain basic forms of grammar and syntax. There is a minimum of formal explanation. Instead, new items of grammar are introduced in each chapter by pattern practice, and are constantly reinforced in succeeding lessons.

A word about the format is in order. An attempt is made to present all lessons in a uniform manner, leading to appropriate exercises and pattern drills throughout the text. This format is used to reinforce the learned material. There is a noticeable gradation in the presentation of all new learning material, varying in degree of sophistication while keeping step with student's progressive acquisition of knowledge and communicative confidence. This process increases the incentive for learning while eliminating boredom and guesswork.

In deference to students not familiar with the Roman alphabet, a preliminary chapter, "Getting Started," touches on penmanship. This is an added feature and serves a "warm-up" for the Copy or Listen and Write exercises that follow in subsequent chapters. Also discussed in this chapter are spelling and syllabification. These are supplementary items and can be omitted when and if a classroom situation so warrants.

The primary objective of Let's Begin is to afford the student a fair level of comprehension as well as expression in American English, both spoken and written. The text undertakes to present learning situations other than those usually encountered in the classroom. For that purpose, a variety of up-to-date short readings and dialogues have been composed. These dialogues give students easy access to everyday and are augmented in each chapter. This method facilitates memorization through repetition.

Each chapter is divided into sections. The heading of the section indicates in simple terms of what the student is to do: Read, Listen/Talk, Copy, Pronunciation Practice, Identify, Complete, Guess Who?, Give the Name, etc. Each section fulfills a specific function within the chapter. Therefore, an attempt should be made to complete all sections. However, the order and extent of coverage of the individual sections is left up to the discretion of the instructor. The section approach makes it possible for the instructor to determine the order of presentation of material best suited for the needs of the students. Each section is constructed in a manner that lends itself to the presentation of the grammatical items which are to be learned within the given chapter, and is properly graded so as not to present material beyond that already studied.

The introductory section, Read, describes a situation which will help the student to understand the grammatical items which are to be learned within the given chapter. The situation also serves to prepare students to personalize and re-create at a later time the dialogue which follows it.

The initial situations and Dialogues are developed to teach a variety of topics. These range from survival skills, such as asking questions about things and people, to riding buses and ordering food in a restaurant or dealing with questions of time and money. The talking materials are designed to help students role-play, using American English in a variety of interactional situations.

The Listen/Talk section is used as a follow-up to the Situation. It provides students with the opportunity to practice the lines of the dialogue aloud, as in role-playing. It further stimulates them to amplify their communicative skill actively, depending on their degree of creative ability and the extent of their progress.

The Listen/ Talk section can be memorized if desired because it is short and conversational in form and it deals with interesting topics relating to everyday life. It is essential that students master both Read and Listen/Talk sections before continuing with the material that follows. Read and Listen/Talk are the core sections of each chapter.

In addition to the Talk, Extra Dialogues are featured in many chapters. These serve to illustrate some point of grammar or emphasize newly learned vocabulary in a practical setting. These short encounters can also be memorized and acted out by students in a classroom. This feature gives the learner an opportunity to personalize the context of the lesson for greater depth of comprehension and ultimate retention of material learned.

The Copy section provides writing practice, especially for those students whose language does not utilize the Roman alphabet as its model for writing. The initial chapters provide patterns to Copy, both in printed and cursive form. Later in the text, as the student becomes accustomed to using the Roman alphabet, the cursive part is left out. Beginning with Chapter 4, some Copy exercises are converted into Listen and Write (dictation) practice.

The listening materials are indicated throughout the text with a drawing of a student wearing headset and listening in a language lab. The drills afford the student additional voice intonation other than that of the classroom instructor. Written exercises test and reinforce student comprehension and progress.

Among other attractive and useful features of Let's Begin are the Unscramble exercises and the Puzzles. These types of exercises serve to emphasize spelling awareness and make it interesting for students to increase their word power.

A familiar American Proverb, illustrated to facilitate comprehension, completes each chapter to further the student's appreciation of life and customs in the United States of America. The overall goal of Let's Begin is to help develop the essential skills of "Zero Plus" knowledge which are a must if the student is to continue on the way to communicative competence in further studies of English. The basic aspects of the language acquired here are: a cultural appreciation, reading comprehension, writing ability, vocabulary building, and conversation. It is hoped that the interesting and timely topics presented here will help make the study of American English a pleasurable experience and one that will encourage the student to further explore our rich language.

Getting Started

IN THIS CHAPTER

The Alphabet

Syllabification

Important Sounds

Penmanship

The Alphabet

Repeat the names of the letters in the alphabet.

CAPITAL	lower case	*Cursive*	*Sound*
A	a	𝒶𝒶	a
B	b	ℬ𝒷	bee
C	c	𝒞𝒸	see
D	d	𝒟𝒹	dee
E	e	ℰℯ	ee
F	f	ℱ𝒻	eff
G	g	𝒢𝑔	gee
H	h	ℋ𝒽	aitch
I	i	ℐ𝒾	i
J	j	𝒥𝒿	jay
K	k	𝒦𝓀	kay
L	l	ℒ𝓁	ell
M	m	ℳ𝓂	emm
N	n	𝒩𝓃	enn
O	o	𝒪𝑜	ou
P	p	𝒫𝓅	pee
Q	q	𝒬𝓆	queue
R	r	ℛ𝓇	ahr
S	s	𝒮𝓈	ess
T	t	𝒯𝓉	tee
U	u	𝒰𝓊	you
V	v	𝒱𝓋	vee
W	w	𝒲𝓌	double-you
X	x	𝒳𝓍	eks
Y	y	𝒴𝓎	why
Z	z	𝒵𝓏	zee

Spelling

Repeat letters aloud.

Dan Carson	D-a-n C-a-r-s-o-n
Gloria Carson	G-l-o-r-i-a C-a-r-s-o-n
Hiromi Naga	H-i-r-o-m-i N-a-g-a
Yukio Naga	Y-u-k-i-o N-a-g-a
Barry Powell	B-a-r-r-y P-o-w-e-l-l
Ethel Powell	E-t-h-e-l P-o-w-e-l-l
Mike Anderson	M-i-k-e A-n-d-e-r-s-o-n
Victoria	V-i-c-t-o-r-i-a
Pedro Flores	P-e-d-r-o F-l-o-r-e-s
Ron Plaza	R-o-n P-l-a-z-a

Writing

Copy these names in cursive writing

Ann Carson	*Ann Carson*
Jane Naga	*Jane Naga*
Donald Powell	*Donald Powell*
Helen Powell	*Helen Powell*
Isaac Anderson	*Isaac Anderson*
Angel Lopez	*Angel Lopez*
Manuel Vargas	*Manuel Vargas*
Alice Hugo	*Alice Hugo*

Syllabification

Repeat syllables aloud. Write complete word.

af-ter-noon	*afternoon*
al-so	*also*
hel-lo	*hello*
caf-e-te-ri-a	*cafeteria*
fa-ther	*father*
host-ess	*hostess*

hun-gry	*hungry*
Ja-pan	*Japan*
lat-er	*later*
morn-ing	*morning*
moth-er	*mother*
on-ly	*only*
par-ents	*parents*
res-tau-rant	*restaurant*
sis-ter	*sister*
stu-dent	*student*
to-day	*today*
Ven-e-zu-e-la	*Venezuela*
wom-an	*woman*

Important Sounds

Repeat aloud.

beet – bit – bet – book – bike – boy
this – these – those – thin – thick
why – when – where – what – who – which
sing – song – thing – morning – evening
is – does – goes – studies – says – reads
keep – eat – even – read – be – key
she – sheep – ship – show – short – shore
child – change – chair – chicken – teacher – watch

Penmanship

Copy each letter or word.

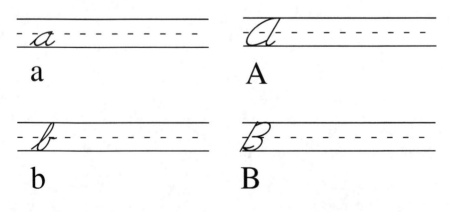

a   A

b   B

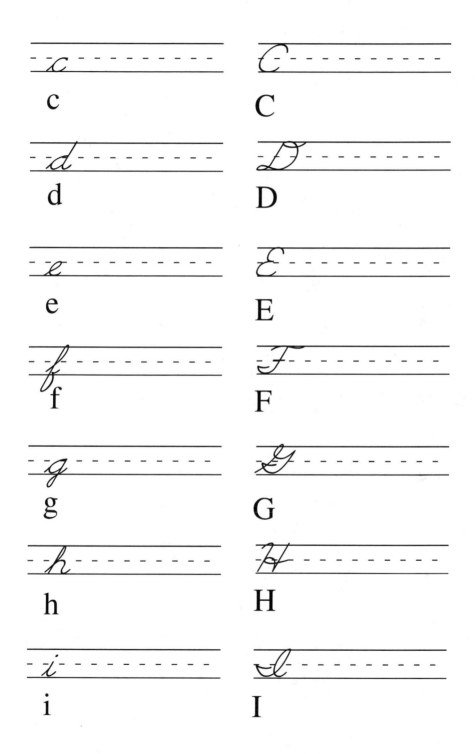

c   C

d   D

e   E

f   F

g   G

h   H

i   I

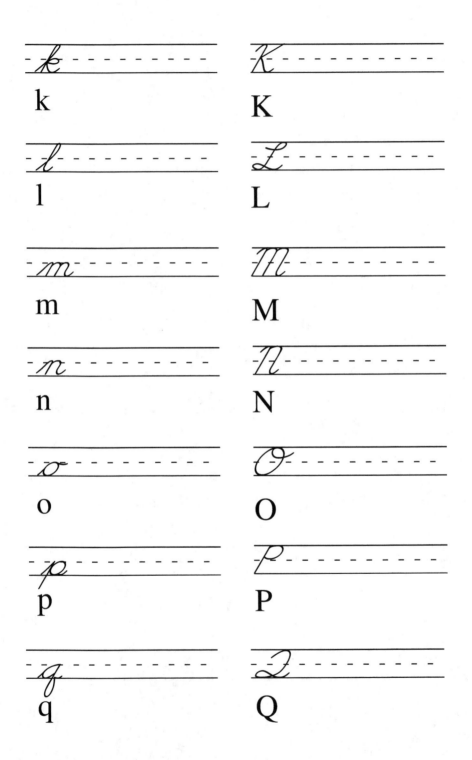

k   K

l   L

m   M

n   N

o   O

p   P

q   Q

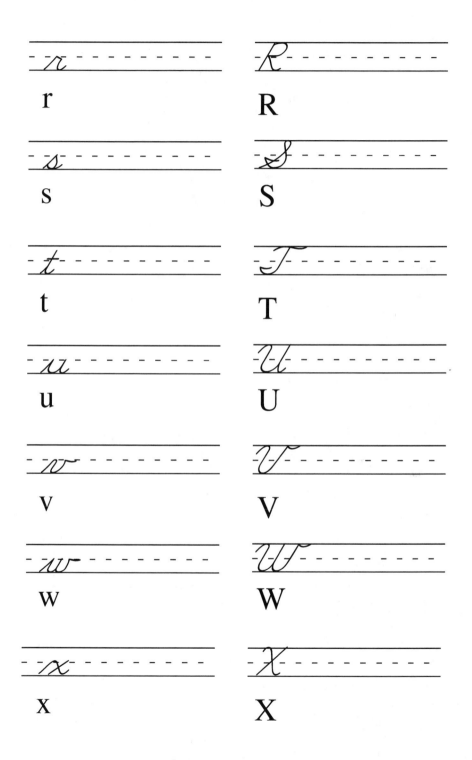

r

R

s

S

t

T

u

U

v

V

w

W

x

X

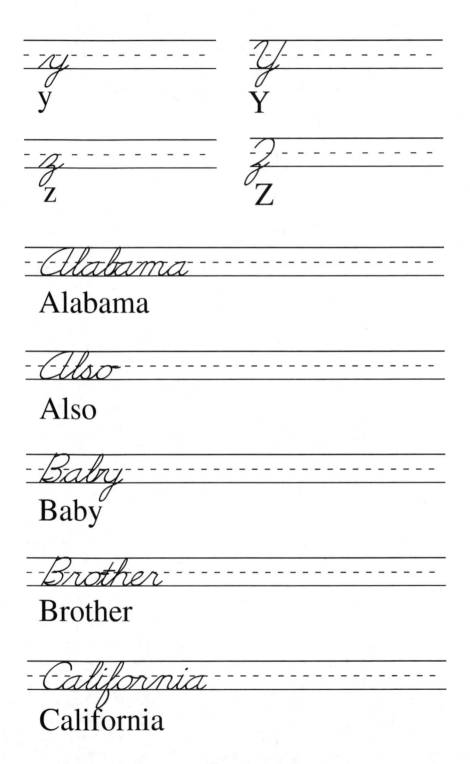

y
Y

z
Z

Alabama
Alabama

Also
Also

Baby
Baby

Brother
Brother

California
California

Come

Come

Daddy

Daddy

Drink

Drink

England

England

Europe

Europe

France

France

Florida

Florida

Geography

Geography

Gum

Gum

Hungry

Hungry

Home

Home

Idaho

Idaho

Inside

Inside

Japan

Japan

Jacket

Jacket

Kleenex

Kleenex

Knife

Knife

Long

Long

Letter

Letter

Matter

Matter

Middle

Middle

North

North

Niece

Niece

Often

Often

Only

Only

Pear

Pear

Potato

Potato

Quick

Quick

Quiet

Quiet

Really

Really

Rise

Rise

Snake

Snake

Strong

Strong

Texas

Texas

Thin

Thin

Umbrella

Umbrella

Under

Under

Very

Very

Visit

Visit

Where

Where

Woman

Woman

Xerox

Xerox

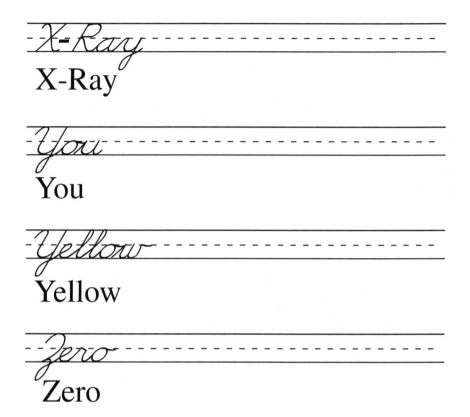

X-Ray

You

Yellow

Zero

CHAPTER ONE

Hello and Goodbye

IN THIS CHAPTER

Questions with *wh* and *is* / *how* and *where*

Present Time of the verbs *to have* and *to be*

Contractions: *we've* / *you've* / *they've*
what's / *it's*, etc.

Affirmative statement: Noun Phrase + Verb Phrase

Demonstratives: *this* / *that*

Singular and Plural

Read

Situation

Hiromi Naga is a student. Hiromi is from Japan. José Betancourt is from Venezuela. José is a student. José has an English class. Hiromi also has an English class. José and Hiromi talk.

Listen/Talk

Dialogue

José:	Hello, Hiromi. How are you?
Hiromi:	I'm fine, thank you. How are you?
José:	Fine, thanks. What's that?
Hiromi:	Oh, it's an English book.
José:	Let's sit a while.
Hiromi:	Not now, here's my ride. See you later, José.
José:	Goodbye, Hiromi. See you soon.

Copy

friends *friends*
hello *hello*
fine *fine*
thank you *thank you*
student *student*
see you *see you*
goodbye *goodbye*

school *school*
How are you? *How are you?*
I'm fine. *I'm fine.*
thanks *thanks*
Are you a student? *Are you a student?*
See you later. *See you later.*
See you soon. *See you soon.*

Repeat—Who Is Who?

This is Hiromi.

Hiromi is a girl.

That's José.

José is a boy.

This is Ann.
She and Hiromi are friends.

That's Donald.
Donald and José are friends.

Donald is a boy,
and José is a boy.
Donald and José are boys.

Hiromi is a girl,
and Ann is a girl.
Hiromi and Ann are girls.

This is Mrs. Naga.

That's Mr. Naga.

This is Mrs. Betancourt.

That's Mr. Betancourt.

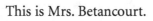

This is Yukio Naga.

That's Isaac Betancourt.

 This is Jane Naga.

That's Victoria Betancourt.

 This is Mr. Carson.
Mr. Carson is a man.

That's Mrs. Carson.
Mrs. Carson is a woman.

 This is Mr. Powell.
Mr. Powell is a man.

That's Mrs. Powell.
Mrs. Powell is a woman.

 This is Ann Carson.
Ann Carson is a girl.

That's Donald Powell.
Donald Powell is a boy.

 This is Mike Anderson.
Mike Anderson is a nurse.

That's Angel Lopez.
Angel Lopez is a TV repairman.

This is Manuel Vargas.

Manuel is a secretary.

That's Alice Hugo.

She's a restaurant hostess.

Copy

girl _girl_   boy _boy_

a girl _a girl_   a boy _a boy_

the girl _the girl_   the boy _the boy_

this girl _this girl_   this boy _this boy_

This is a girl. _This is a girl._   This is a boy. _This is a boy._

This is the girl. _This is the girl._   This is the boy. _This is the boy._

student _student_   school _school_

a student _a student_   a school _a school_

the student _the student_   the school _the school_

this student _this student_   this school _this school_

This is a student. _This is a student._   This is a school. _This is a school._

This is the student. _This is the student._   This is the school. _This is the school._

friend _friend_   woman _woman_

a friend _a friend_   a woman _a woman_

the friend _the friend_   the woman _the woman_

this friend _this friend_   this woman _this woman_

This is a friend. _This is a friend._   This is a woman. _This is a woman._

This is the friend. _This is the friend._   This is the woman. _This is the woman._

Pronunciation Practice

Words

girl	a girl	the girl	this girl
boy	a boy	the boy	this boy
man	a man	the man	that man
woman	a woman	the woman	that woman
student	a student	the student	this student
school	a school	the school	this school
friend	a friend	the friend	that friend
school	a school	the school	that school

Statements

This is a girl.   That's a boy.

This is the girl.   That's the boy.

This is a student.   That's a school.

This is the student.   That's the school.

This is a friend.   That's a woman.

This is the friend.   That's the woman.

Questions with wh- and is

Who is this?—Is this Hiromi?

Who is this?—Is this the teacher?

Who is this?—Is this the woman?

Who is this?—Is this the boy?

Who is this?—Is this the girl?

What's this?—It's a book.

What's this?—It's a classroom.

What's that?—That's the English class.

What's that?—It's the lab.

How are you?—I'm fine, thanks.

How's Hiromi?—Oh, I don't know.

How is it?—It's O.K., thank you.

Identify—Who Is Who?

Who is this?

This is Hiromi.

Who is this?

This is José.

Who is this?

This is Ann.

Who is this?

This is Donald.

Who is this?

This is Mrs. Naga.

Who is this?

This is Mr. Naga.

Who is this?

This is Yukio.

Who is this?

This is Jane.

Who is this?

This is Mrs. Betancourt.

Who is this?

This is Mr. Betancourt.

Who is this?

This is Isaac.

Who is this?

This is Victoria.

Study

Present Time of **to have**

I have	We have (we've)
You have	You have (you've)
He She } has It	They have (they've)

The contractions *we've, you've, they've* are used in conversation only; also *what's* for *what is*, and *it's* for *it is*.

Present Time of **to be**

I am (I'm)	We are (we're)
You are (You're)	You are (you're)
He is (he's) She is (she's) } It is (it's)	They are (they're)

I'm is a contraction of *I am*. All contractions are used in conversation only.

Affirmative Statements

<u>Noun Phrase</u>	<u>Plus</u>	<u>Verb Phrase</u>
Hiromi		is a girl.
José		is a student.
She		is a girl.
This		is Ann.
Ann		is a girl.
He		is a boy.

Questions With **is**

Is comes first in a question. The answer is *yes* or *no*.

Is Hiromi a student?—Yes, she is a student.
Is Yukio from Japan?—Yes, he is from Japan.

Is Isaac from Venezuela?—Yes, Isaac is from Venezuela.
Is Ann from the U.S.A.?—Yes, Ann is from the U.S.A.

Questions With who

Who is Hiromi?—Hiromi is a student.
Who is José?—José is a student.
Who are Hiromi and José?—Hiromi and José are students.
Who is Jane?—Jane is the travel guide.

Questions With what

What is this?—It's a restaurant.
What's this?—It's a classroom.
What's that?—That is a school.
What's that?—That's a cafeteria.

Questions With where / how

Where are you from?—I'm from Japan.
Where is he from?—He's from Venezuela.
Where's Ann from?—Ann's from the U.S.A.

How are you?—Thanks, I'm fine.
How's your friend?—Oh, I don't know.
How's José?—He's fine, thanks.

Practice

Contractions

I *am* Mr. Carson. I*'m* a lawyer.
You *are* from Japan. You*'re* a student.
This *is* José. He*'s* from Venezuela.
This *is* Ann. She*'s* also a student.

We *are* friends. We'*re* students.
Hiromi and José *are* friends.
I *am* Mr. Powell. I'*m* a teacher.
Mr. and Mrs. Powell *are* hosts.

Verb to be

Fill in the missing *to be* form:

Example: Hiromi ____is____ from Japan.

1. I _____ Mr. Carson.

2. This _____ Hiromi.

3. We _____ friends.

4. They _____ students.

5. Hiromi _____ a girl.

6. José _____ a boy.

7. Victoria _____ a woman.

8. Isaac _____ a man.

9. Isaac and José _____ brothers.

10. Mr. and Mrs. Powell _____ hosts.

11. Yukio _____ from Japan.

12. Jane and Hiromi _____ sisters.

Substitution

Substitute the word *is* or *are* in the sentences below. Copy the complete sentence.

Example: I am a student.

She _____

She *is* a student.

We _____

We *are* students.

Ann is a student.

She _____

Isaac is a man.

He _____

José is from Venezuela.

He _____

José and Hiromi are friends.

They _____

Ann is also a student.

She _____

Victoria is from Venezuela.

She _____

Mrs. Carson is a lawyer.

She _____

Mrs. Naga is from Japan.

She _____

Miss Powell is a reporter.

She _____

Unscramble

Unscramble the letters to make words.

Example: ___afther___ = ___father___

owh _____   lrig _____

woh _____   ese _____

rea _____   yuo _____

ehs _____   mofr _____

oyb _____   ohlel _____

Answers to Unscramble: who; how; she; boy; girl; see; you; from; hello

Substitution

Substitute the *noun phrase* or the *verb phrase* into the statement.

Examples: Hiromi is a student.
She's <u>a student.</u>
José is a boy.
He's <u>a boy.</u>

is a boy _____

José _____

Victoria _____

Ann _____

Isaac _____

Isaac and José _____

Ann and Hiromi _____

are friends _____

is a girl _____

are sisters _____

Pronunciation

Pronounce the underlined words and answer the questions.

<u>boy</u>   Who is a boy? (José) _____

<u>girl</u>   Who is a girl? (Hiromi) _____

<u>hungry</u> Who's hungry? (José and Hiromi) _____

<u>idea</u>   Who has an idea? (Hiromi) _____

<u>student</u> Is Hiromi a student? (Yes) _____

<u>class</u>   Who has an English class? (Hiromi and José) _____

_____

Change Statements to Questions

Change the following statements to *yes/no* questions.

Example: Hiromi is a girl. = <u>Is Hiromi a girl?</u>

This is Ann. _____

He is a boy. _____

This is Donald. _____

She is a girl. _____

This is Mr. Carson. _____

José is a student. _____

This is Helen. _____

He's a student. _____

Hiromi is a student. _____

Write Questions

Make who questions. Follow the example.

Example: <u>José—Who's José?</u>

Hiromi _____? Ann _____?

José _____? Isaac _____?

She _____? he _____?

Victoria _____? a student _____?

Substitution Drill

1. Hello, **Hiromi.**

      Ann.

      José.

      Victoria.

      Isaac.

2. Good morning, **José**.
     Ann.
     Mr. Powell.
     Dr. Carson.

3. Hello, **José**. How are you?
   Isaac.
   Ann.
   Mr. Powell.

4. Hello, Mr. Powell. How are you **today?**
        this morning?
        this afternoon?
        this evening?

5. I'm **fine**, thank you, and you?
   O.K.,
   very well,
   pretty well,
   a little tired.

6. Are you **O.K.?**
     well?
     tired?

7. Here's my **ride.**
     friend.
     brother.
     sister.

8. See you **later**, José.
    this afternoon.
    this evening.

9. Goodbye, **Hiromi**. See you soon.
    José.
    Ann.
    Isaac.

Complete the READING using the words below.

are   is

Hiromi and José _____ friends. Hiromi _____ from Japan. José _____ from Venezuela. Hiromi and José _____ friends. Hiromi and José _____ at school. They talk.

Complete the TALK using the words below.

see you later   goodbye   see you soon   student   ride
                    I'm fine   How are you

José: Hello, Hiromi. _____ ?

Hiromi: _____ thank you. _____ ?

José: Fine, thanks. Are you a _____ ?

Hiromi: Yes, I am. And you?

José: I'm also a _____ .

Hiromi: Oh, here's my _____ . _____, José.

José: _____ , Hiromi. _____ .

Copy

friend *friend* _____ Hiromi and José are friends. *Hiromi and José are friends.*

from *from* _____ She is from Japan. *She is from Japan.*

school *school* _____ Is this a school? *Is this a school?*

talk *talk* _____ José and Hiromi talk. *José and Hiromi talk.*

he *he* _____ Is he a student? *Is he a student?*

she *she* _____ Is she the girl? *Is she the girl?*

sister *sister* _____ Isaac and José are brothers. *Isaac and José are brothers.*

brother _brother_   Yukio and Hiromi are brother and sister. _Yukio and Hiromi are brother and sister._

who _who_   Who is this? _Who is this?_

how _how_   How are you? _How are you?_

see _see_   See you later (soon). _See you later (soon)._

here _here_   Is he here? _Is he here?_

ride _ride_   There's my ride. _There's my ride._

Exercises

Guess Who

Answer *yes* or *no* with a *complete* sentence.

Is this Mr. Naga?

_____

Is this Hiromi?

_____

Is this José?

_____

Is this Jane?

_____

Is this Mrs. Betancourt?

_____

Is this Donald?

_____

Is this Victoria?

_____

Give the Name

Answer with a *complete* statement.

Who is this?

Is it _____ ?

_____

Who is this?

Is it _____ ?

_____

Who is this?

Is it _____ ?

_____

Who is this?

Is it _____ ?

_____

Who is this?

Is it _____ ?

_____

Who is this?

Is it _____ ?

_____

Who is this?

Is it _____ ?

_____

Who is this?

Is it _____ ?

_____

Who is this?

Is it _____ ?

_____

Who is this?

Is it _____ ?

_____

Who is this?

Is it _____ ?

_____

Tell Your Friend

Example: your *name.*

My name is _____ .

1. about José and Hiromi

_____

2. where Hiromi is from

_____

3. where José is from

_____

4. where Hiromi and José are from

_____

5. what the teacher's name is

_____

6. how you are

_____

7. that your ride is here

_____

8. you'll see him/her soon

_____

Writing

Write a situation about the following dialogue.

Hiromi: Hello, José. How are you?
José: I'm fine, thank you. How are you?
Hiromi: Fine, thanks. Only, I'm very hungry.
José: Let's go to the cafeteria.
Hiromi: That's a good idea.
José: Here comes the bus. Get in!

Proverb

A hard beginning makes a good ending. (In the beginning it is more difficult to do things but we are happy to finish what we start out.)

CHAPTER TWO

Meet My Friends

IN THIS CHAPTER

Negatives—*no / not*

Personal Pronoun Subjects:
I/you/he/she/it/we/you/they

Demonstrative Pronouns: *this /that
here / there*—Questions with *what*

Negative contractions: *isn't/aren't*

Nationalities

Read

Situation

This is the Carson home. We are having a party. All our friends are here. Mr. Carson is a lawyer. His wife is a doctor. This is where Hiromi Naga lives. Ann Carson and Hiromi are friends. Ann's also a student. There is Mr. Powell. He's a teacher. José Betancourt lives with the Powells. There are many people at the party.

There's Donald Powell and Mrs. Powell. Mrs. Powell is an auto mechanic. José has a sister. Her name is Victoria. She and her brother Isaac are here on a visit. Mike Anderson is a nurse at the hospital. José and Hiromi are friends. Manuel Vargas is a secretary. He and Hiromi are friends.

Listen/Talk

Dialogue

Mr. Carson: Pardon me, aren't you Ethel Powell?
Victoria: No, I'm not. I'm Victoria Betancourt.
Mrs. Carson: José talks about you often.

Mr. Carson: Is that Mr. Powell?
Victoria: Yes, it is. Let me introduce you . . . Mr. Carson, this is
               Mr. Powell.
Mr. Carson: Nice to meet you.
Mr. Powell: I'm glad to meet you.
Victoria: Let's have another drink.
Ann: Sure, let's go and get one.

Copy

a home _a home_   have _have_

a party _a party_   having _having_

we are _we are_   We're having a party. _We're having a party._

introduce _introduce_   may I _may I_

May I introduce . . . ? _May I introduce . . . ?_

glad _glad_   Glad to meet you. _Glad to meet you._

she's _she's_   She's a doctor. _She's a doctor._

he's _he's_   He's a teacher. _He's a teacher._

she's here _she's here_   on a visit _on a visit_

She's here on a visit. _She's here on a visit._

Repeat—Who Is Who

This is Mrs. Carson.
Mrs. Carson is a doctor.

This is Mr. Carson.
Mr. Carson is a lawyer.

This is Hiromi.
Hiromi is a student.

This is Manuel.
Manuel and Hiromi are friends.
Manuel is a secretary.

This is Jane.
Jane is a travel guide. She
and Hiromi are sisters.

This is Yukio.
He and Jane are brother and
sister. Yukio's a car salesman. Jane
and Yukio are in Japan.
They are not at the party.

This is Mr. Powell.
He's a professor.

This is Mrs. Powell.
She's an auto mechanic.
Hiromi lives with the Powells.

This is Sally Jones.
She studies chemistry.

This is José.
José studies engineering.
Ann and José like the party.

This is Alice Hugo.
She's a waitress.

This is Mike Anderson.
Mike is a nurse.
Alice and Mike are at work.

This is Mr. Naga.
He sells bicycles.

This is Mrs. Naga.
She's a housewife.
They are not at the party.

This is Isaac.
Isaac is a soccer player.

This is Victoria.
Victoria is a hair stylist.
Isaac and Victoria are not at the party.

This is Helen Powell.
She's a newspaper reporter.

This is Angel Lopez.
He works in
a TV repair shop.
He's a TV repairman.

Copy

doctor _doctor_ a doctor _a doctor_

the doctor _the doctor_ this is _this is_

This is Doctor Carson. _This is Doctor Carson._

lawyer _lawyer_ a lawyer _a lawyer_

the lawyer _the lawyer_ that is _that is_

That is Mr. Carson, the lawyer. _That is Mr. Carson, the lawyer._

travel _travel_ guide _guide_ she's _she's_

She's a travel guide. _She's a travel guide._

waitress _waitress_ a waitress _a waitress_

the waitress _the waitress_ Alice _Alice_

Alice is a waitress. _Alice is a waitress._

work _work_ at work _at work_

Alice _Alice_ Mike _Mike_

Alice and Mike are at work. _Alice and Mike are at work._

bicycle _bicycle_ a bicycle _a bicycle_

the bicycle _the bicycle_ Mr. Naga _Mr. Naga_

Mr. Naga sells bicycles. _Mr. Naga sells bicycles._

hair _hair_ stylist _stylist_

a hair stylist _a hair stylist_

Victoria is a hair stylist. _Victoria is a hair stylist._

Pronunciation Practice

Words

home	a home	the home
party	a party	the party
doctor	a doctor	the doctor
lawyer	a lawyer	the lawyer

Questions	*Statements*
Is she a doctor?	She's a doctor.
Is he a lawyer?	He's a lawyer.
Is Manuel a secretary?	He's a secretary.
Is Jane a travel guide?	She's a travel guide.
Is Mr. Powell a professor?	He's a professor.
Is Ann a chemistry student?	She's a chemistry student.
Is José an engineering student?	José is an engineering student.
Is Alice a waitress?	Alice is a waitress.
Is Mike a nurse?	He's a nurse.
Is Mr. Naga a bicycle salesman?	He's a bicycle salesman.

Questions	*Answers*
Who's a doctor?	Mrs. Carson is a doctor.
Who's a lawyer?	Mr. Carson is a lawyer.
Who's a student?	Hiromi is a student.
Who's a secretary?	Manuel is a secretary.
Who's a travel guide?	Jane is a travel guide.
Who's a salesman?	Yukio is a salesman.
Who's an auto mechanic?	Mrs. Powell is an auto mechanic.
Who's an engineering student?	José is an engineering student.
Who's a waitress?	Alice is a waitress.
Who's a nurse?	Mike is a nurse.
Who's a housewife?	Mrs. Naga is a housewife.
Who's a soccer player?	Isaac is a soccer player.
Who's a newspaper reporter?	Helen is a newspaper reporter.

Let Me Introduce . . .

Ann, this is Jane.

    Jane, this is Ann.

Manuel, this is Mr. Powell.

    Mr. Powell, this is Manuel.

Isaac, this is Victoria.

    Victoria, this is Isaac.

Dan, this is Alice.
Gloria, this is Manuel.
Hiromi, this is Angel.
Yukio, this is Mike.
Jane, this is Helen.
Mr. Naga, this is Dr. Carson.
Mrs. Naga, this is Dr. Powell.
Mrs. Powell, this is José.
Isaac, this is Ann.
Victoria, this is Donald.
Helen, this is Mike.

Identify—Who Is Who?

Who is this?
Is he a lawyer?
Is he Ann's father?
Is he American?

This is Mr. Carson.
Yes, he's a lawyer.
He's Ann's father.
He's American.

Who is this?
Is she a doctor?
Is she Mr. Carson's wife?
Is she American?

This is Mrs. Carson.
Yes, she's a doctor.
Yes, she is.
She's also American.

Who is that?
Is she a nurse?

Is she from Japan?
Is she Japanese?

That's Hiromi.
No, she's not a nurse.
Hiromi is a student.
She's from Japan.
She's Japanese.

Who is that?
Is she a hair stylist?

Is she American?

That's Mrs. Powell.
No, she's not a hair stylist.
She's an auto mechanic.
She's American.

Who's this?
Is he a student?

Is he from Venezuela?
Is he Venezuelan?

This is José.
Yes, he is.
José is a student.
He's from Venezuela.
He's Venezuelan.

Who's that?
Is she José's sister?

Is she Venezuelan?

That's Victoria.
Yes, she is.
Victoria is José's sister.
She's from Venezuela.
She's also Venezuelan.

Who's this?
Is he a nurse?

Is he from Mexico?
Is he Mexican?

This is Mike.
Yes, he is.
Mike is a nurse.
He's from Mexico.
He's Mexican.

Who's that?
Is she a soccer player?
Is she French?

That's Alice.
No, she is a waitress.
Yes, she is French.

Who's this?
Is he an auto mechanic?

This is Angel Lopez.
No, he's not an
auto mechanic.
He's a TV repairman.

Is he from Argentina?

No, he's from Spain.
He's Spanish.

Who's that?
Is he a salesman?
Is he from the U.S.A.?

That's Mr. Naga.
Yes, he's a salesman.
No, he's from Japan.
He's Japanese.

Study

Negatives

Is he a nurse?
Is she a doctor?
Is he Mexican?
Is she from Japan?

no / not

—No, he's not. He's a TV repairman.
—No, she's not. She's a hair stylist.
—No, he's not. He's American.
—No, she's not. She's from Venezuela.

Personal Pronoun Subjects
I/you/he/she/it/we/they

*I'*m Gloria Carson.
Are *you* Manuel Vargas?
No, *I'*m not.
*He'*s Manuel. *I'*m Angel Lopez.

*I'*m Victoria Betancourt.
Are *you* Helen Powell?
No, *I'*m not.
*She'*s Helen Powell. *I'*m Ann Carson.

Is that the hospital?
Yes, *it* is.

We are from Mexico.
Are *they* from Japan?
Yes, *they* are.

This/That

Is *this* Mr. Naga?
Yes, it is.

Is *that* Mrs. Carson?
No, *that's* not Mrs. Carson.
That's Mrs. Powell.

Is *this* Manuel Vargas?
Yes, it is.

Is *that* Angel Lopez?
No, *that's* not Angel. *That's* Mike Anderson.

Here/There

Here is Mrs. Naga.
Who is *there*?
There is Mr. Naga.

Knock! Knock!
Who's *there*?
Mr. Carson's *here*.
Come in, Mr. Carson.

Here are my friends Mike and Manuel.
Who's at school?
Many students are *there*.

Questions With what
What is it?
Oh, it's nothing.

What's happening?
Nothing much.

What is she?
She's a nurse.

What is Hiromi?
Hiromi is a student.

What is it?
It's a bicycle.

Negative Contractions—isn't/aren't
Isn't it Alice?—No, it *isn't* Alice. It's Victoria.
Isn't it Manuel?—Yes, it's Manuel.
Aren't you Ann?—No, I'm not. I'm Helen.
Aren't they friends?—No, they *aren't*.

Practice

Negatives—no/not
Is this a Japanese restaurant?
No, this is *not* a Japanese restaurant. It's a . . .

Are you Mr. Carson?
No, I'm *not* Mr. Carson. I'm . . .

Is she a nurse?
No, she's *not* a nurse. She's . . .

Is he a TV repairman?
No, he's *not* a TV repairman. He's . . .

Is this an English class?
No, this is *not* an English class. This is . . .

Is that Mrs. Naga?
No, that's *not* Mrs. Naga. That's . . .

Are they your friends?
No, they're *not* my friends. They're . . .

Personal Pronouns
I/you/he/she/it/we/they

I'm Mr. Carson. Are *you* Mr. Vargas?
No, *I*'m not Mr. Vargas. *He's* Mr. Vargas.

He's a nurse. Is *she* also a nurse?
No, *she's* not a nurse. *She's* a doctor.

Who's talking with Mrs. Naga?
It's Manuel Vargas.

Is that Mrs. Naga?
Yes, *it* is.

We are from the U.S.A.
Where are you from? *We* are from Argentina.

They are from Japan. Are *they* students?
Yes, *they* are.—No, *they* aren't.

This/That

This is Gloria. Who's *that*?
That's Victoria. Who's *this*?
This is Hiromi and *that's* Alice.
Is *that* Alice? Yes, *that's* Alice.
Who's talking with Gloria?—Oh, *that's* Manuel.

Here/There

Is Manuel *there*? Yes, he's *here*.
Here's Alice. Who's *there*?
There are many friends at the party. Who's at the party?
Many people are *there*. *There* is Yukio.
Is José *there*? Yes, he is *here*.
There are also Mike, and Angel, and Helen.

What

What's this? This is a car. (book, party, house, etc.)
What's that? That's a bicycle. (TV, hospital, room, etc.)
What's there? Oh, I don't know.
What's this? This is a lab. (school, cafeteria, drink, etc.)
What's that? That's Hiromi's book. (bicycle, class, bus, etc.)
What's is it? It's a book. (table, drink, piano, etc.)
What is it? It's a bicycle. (restaurant, car, classroom, etc.)

Negative Contractions
isn't/aren't

Isn't this Alice? (Manuel, Victoria, Hiromi, etc.)
Isn't that a bicycle? (car, TV, restaurant, etc.)
Isn't she from Japan? (Venezuela, France, Mexico, etc.)
Isn't he American? (Venezuelan, French, Mexican, etc.)
Isn't it Hiromi's ride? (book, class, brother, etc.)

Aren't they Hiromi's friends? (parents, relatives, etc.)
Aren't they from France? (Mexico, Venezuela, etc.)
Aren't they Mexican? (French, American, etc.)

Substitution Drill

	a lawyer?		a lawyer.
	a professor?		a professor.
Are you	a nurse?	I'm (am) not	a nurse.
Aren't you	a mechanic?	He isn't (is not)	a mechanic.
Is he/she	a secretary?	She isn't (is not)	a secretary.
Isn't he/she	a hostess?		a hostess.
	an engineer?		an engineer.
	a soccer player?		a soccer player.

		lawyer.	
		professor.	
		student.	Mexican.
		nurse.	French.
I'm	a/an	mechanic.	American.
I'm not	a/an	soccer player.	Venezuelan.
		newspaper reporter.	Japanese.
		secretary.	
		hostess.	
		engineer.	

Pardon me, **Manuel.**

Excuse me, **Ann.**
       Mr. Carson.
       Hiromi.
       José.

Are you **Lisa Solis?**
        Angel Lopez?
        Manuel Vargas?
        Alice Hugo?
        Ron Plaza?

Are you from **France?**
        Mexico?
        Venezuela?
        the U.S.A.?
        Japan?

Is he **Japanese?**
        French?
        American?
        Venezuelan?
        Mexican?

Is Ann a **mechanic?**
        student?
        nurse?
        lawyer?
        doctor?

I'm glad to meet you, **Mr. Carson.**

Nice to meet you, **Manuel.**
        Hiromi.
        José.
        Mr. Naga.

Copy

car _car_   Yukio sells cars. _Yukio sells cars._

class _class_   That's an English class. _That's an English class._

teacher _teacher_   He's the teacher. _He's the teacher._

live _live_   Hiromi lives here. _Hiromi lives here._

stylist _stylist_   She's a hair stylist. _She's a hair stylist._

party _party_   They're having a party. _They're having a party._

Exercises

Fill in the Blanks

Fill in *this/that/is/'s*

Is _____ Mr. Naga?

No, _____ is Mr. Carson.

Isn't _____ Manuel over there?

Yes, that _____ Manuel.

Fill in *what*

    Example: Helen Powell (a newspaper reporter)

        What's Helen Powell?

    Helen Powell's a newspaper reporter.

        What is she?

        She's a newspaper reporter.

        Manuel   (secretary)

        Alice   (restaurant hostess)

        Donald   (student)

        Victoria   (hair stylist)

        Isaac   (soccer player)

Fill in *who*

Example: Who's that?
That's Mr. Carson.

Who is it?
It's Mr. Carson.

Mr. Naga	(this)
Mrs. Carson	(this)
Helen	(that)
Mike	(that)
Donald	(this)

Fill in the *Nationality*

Example: Hiromi is from (Japan)
Hiromi is <u>Japanese.</u>

José is from Venezuela.

José is _____ .

Manuel is from Mexico.

Manuel is _____ .

Alice is from France.

Alice is _____ .

Mrs. Carson is from America.

Mrs. Carson is _____ .

Mr. Naga is from Japan.

Mr. Naga is _____ .

Hiromi is also from Japan.

Hiromi is also _____ .

Unscramble

Unscramble the letters to make words.

Example: sloa = also

rac _____   kobo _____

dlag _____   riah _____

kile _____   evli _____

yamn _____   korw _____

fiwe _____   rues _____

Answers to Unscramble:

car; book; glad; hair; like; live; many; work; wife; sure

Change Statements to Questions

Change the following statements to *yes/no* questions.

Example: Hiromi is Japanese. = Is Hiromi Japanese?

Manuel is Mexican. _____

Ann is American. _____

José is Venezuelan. _____

Alice is French. _____

Yukio is Japanese. _____

Example: Hiromi is not a nurse. = Isn't Hiromi a nurse?

Manuel is not a student. _____

Ann is not a doctor. _____

Mr. Carson is not a mechanic. _____

Mrs. Powell is not a secretary. _____

Alice is not a nurse. _____

Example: That's Mrs. Naga. = <u>Is that Mrs. Naga?</u>

That's Ann. _____

That's José. _____

That's Mr. Naga. _____

That's Mrs. Carson. _____

That's Mr. Powell. _____

Example: This is from Japan. = <u>Is this from Japan?</u>

This is from Mexico. _____

This is from America. _____

This is from France. _____

This is from Venezuela. _____

This is from Argentina. _____

Example: Here's Mr. Naga. = <u>Who's here?</u>
There's Manuel. = <u>Who's there?</u>

Here's Yukio. _____

Here's Ann. _____

There's Mike. _____

There's Alice. _____

Here's Mrs. Powell. _____

Completion

Complete the reading using the words below.

are there here this a

_____ is the Carson home. We _____ having a party. All our friends are _____ . _____ is where Hiromi lives. _____ is Mr. Powell. He's _____ teacher. There _____ many friends at the party.

Complete the talk using the words below.

let   that   indeed   I'm   pardon   is

you're   nice   glad   not   this

José: _____ me, aren't you Angel Lopez?

Donald: No, I'm _____ . _____ Donald Powell.

José: Oh! So _____ Ann's brother!

Donald: _____ I am.

José: Is _____ Mr. Naga?

Donald: Yes, it _____ . _____ me introduce you . . .

José Betancourt _____ is Mr. Naga.

Mr. Naga: _____ to meet you.

José: I'm _____ to meet you too.

Exercises

Guess What?

Tell the nationality.

This is José.

What is he?

José is _____

This is Hiromi.

What is she?

Hiromi is _____

This is Manuel.

What is he?

Manuel is _____

This is Ann.
What is she?
Ann is _____

This is Mr. Naga.
What is he?
Mr. Naga is _____

This is Alice.
What is she?
Alice is _____

This is Victoria.
What is she?
Victoria is _____

Writing

Write a situation about the following dialogue.

Manuel: Pardon me, are you Yukio?

Yukio: Yes, I'm Yukio Naga.

Manuel: Aren't you from Japan?

Yukio: Yes, I'm Japanese.

Manuel: Are you a student here?

Yukio: I'm an engineering student.

Write a dialogue about the following situation.

You meet someone.
Introduce yourself.
Ask her/his name.
She/he tells you her/his name.
Tell her/him you're from Mexico.
Ask where she's/he's from.
Tell her/him it's nice to meet her/him.

Proverb

Progress is slow. (We learn things step by step.)

CHAPTER THREE

See You at 7 o'Clock

IN THIS CHAPTER

GRAMMATICAL SUMMARY

Possessive Adjectives: *my/your/his/her*
our/your/their

Present Continuous of Verbs
be + *Verb* + *ing*

Numbers 0 (zero) to 20 (twenty)

Telling time—*when?/early/late/on time/*
o'clock/always/never/today

Read

Situation

Mike and Alice are talking during their school break. School is out early today. Mr. Powell, their history professor, is sick. History is always the last period. Mike's ride sometimes comes to pick him up early. But his ride is late today. Mike is taking a bus. Alice and Mike are happy there is no history class. But they are sad because Mr. Powell is sick.

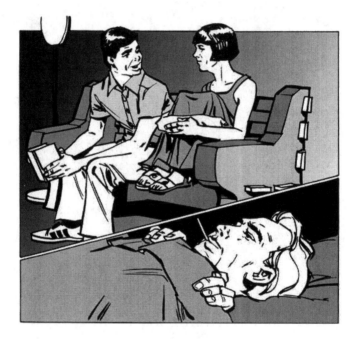

Listen/Talk

Dialogue

Alice: What time is it?

Mike: It's a quarter past three.

Alice: We're getting out early today. How do you like that?

Mike: Great! What are you doing tonight?

Alice: Oh, I don't know.

Mike: There's no homework today. How about a movie?

Alice: O.K. See you at my house around seven o'clock.

Copy

Mike _Mike_ and Alice _and Alice_

Mike and Alice _Mike and Alice_

his _his_ ride _ride_ late _late_

today _today_ but _but_ is _is_

But his ride _But his ride_

is late today _is late today_

But his ride is late today. _But his ride is late today._

what _what_ time _time_ is it _is it_

What time is it? _What time is it?_

It's _It's_ a quarter _a quarter_ past three _past three_

It's a quarter past three. _It's a quarter past three._

Pronunciation Practice

Words

school	a school	the school	
break	a break	the break	
out	early	today	
sick	always	period	
ride	comes	sometimes	late
today	happy	history	class

Questions

Who's talking?

When are they talking?

What's out early today?

Who's sick?

What's the last period?

What comes early sometimes?

What's late today?

What's Mike taking?

Why are Alice and Mike happy?

Why are Mike and Alice sad?

What time is it?

When's school out?

When are you coming?

When's Mike coming?

Statements

Mike and Alice are talking.

They are talking during school break.

School's out early today.

Mr. Powell's sick.

History's the last period.

Mike's ride comes early.

Mike's ride is late today.

Mike's taking a bus.

There is no history class.

Mr. Powell's sick.

It's nine o'clock.

School's out at four o'clock.

I'm coming at seven o'clock.

He's coming at five-thirty.

Questions

Are Mike and Alice talking?

Mike and Alice are talking, aren't they?

Aren't Mike and Alice talking?

Who's talking?

Are they talking during school break?

They're talking during school break, aren't they?

Answers

Yes, Mike and Alice are talking.

No, they aren't. (Yes, they are.)

No, Mike and Alice aren't talking.

Mike and Alice are talking.

Yes, they're talking during school break.

Yes, they are. (No, they aren't.)

Questions	*Answers*
Aren't they talking during school break?	No, they're not talking during school break.
When are they talking?	They're talking during school break.
Is school out early today?	Yes, school's out early today.
School's out early today, isn't it?	No, it isn't. (Yes, it is.)
Isn't school out early today?	No, school's not out early today.
What's out early today?	School's out early today.
Is Mr. Powell the history professor?	Yes, Mr. Powell is the history professor.
Mr. Powell's the history professor, isn't he?	Yes, he is. (No, he isn't.)
Isn't Mr. Naga the history professor?	No, Mr. Naga's not the history professor.
Who's the history professor?	Mr. Powell's the history professor.
Is math the last period?	Yes, math is the last period.
History's the last period, isn't it?	Yes, it is. (No, it isn't.)
Isn't history the last period?	No, history isn't the last period.
What's the last period?	History's the last period.
Is Mike's ride late today?	Yes, Mike's ride is late today.
Mike's ride is late today, isn't it?	Yes, it is. (No, it isn't.)
Isn't Mike's ride late today?	No, Mike's ride is not late today.
What's late today?	Mike's ride is late today.
Is Mike taking a bus?	Yes, Mike is taking a bus.
Mike's taking a bus, isn't he?	Yes, he is. (No, he's not [he isn't].)
Isn't Mike taking a bus?	No, Mike's not taking a bus.
Who's taking a bus?	Mike's taking a bus.
Are Jane and Donald happy?	Yes, Jane and Donald are happy.
Mike and Alice are happy, aren't they?	Yes, they are. (No, they aren't [they're not].)
Aren't Alice and Mike happy?	No, Mike and Alice aren't happy.
Who's happy?	Alice and Mike are happy.
Mr. Powell's sick, isn't he?	Yes, he is. (No, he isn't [he's not].)
Is Mr. Powell sick?	Yes, Mr. Powell's sick.
Isn't Mr. Naga sick?	No, Mr. Naga isn't sick.
Who's sick?	Mr. Powell's sick.

Grammatical Summary

Affirmative—Negative Statement

PRONOUN SUBJECT	PRESENT TIME OF BE	CONTRACTIONS (OF PRONOUN SUBJECTS)	COMPLEMENT
I	am	I'm	a student
			a teacher
You	are	You're	sick—happy
			early—late
He (José)		He's (José's)	Venezuelan—friend
She (Helen)	is	She's (Gloria's)	a nurse—father
			American—cousin
			here
			there
It		It's	my ride
			a classroom
This	is	(not)	José's teacher
			Hiromi's brother
That		That's	Mr. Powell.

Questions and Answers

	there?	Hiromi's there.
	this?	It's José.
Who's (is)	here?	Mrs. Powell's here.
	he?	He's my friend.
	she?	She's a nurse.

What's (is)	that?		That's a classroom.
	this?		This is my book.
	her name?		Her name's Ann.
	your name?		My name's José.
	there?		There's the party.

Is(n't)	it Alice?		it's (not) Alice.
	it nice?		it's (not) nice.
	it my class?	Yes	it's (not) your class.
	it his teacher?	No	it's (not) his teacher.
	it her brother?		it's (not) his brother.
	it Mr. Naga?		it's (not) Mr. Naga.
	it a nurse?		it's (not) a nurse.

Possessive Adjectives
your/his/her/our/your/their/my

1. This is *my* friend.
   Is that *your* brother?
   No, it's *his* cousin.
   Is he also *her* cousin?
   Yes, she's *my* sister and he's *our* cousin.
   Where is *your* English class?
   Over there, next to *their* classroom.

2. Meet my friend, Ann.
       Pleased to meet you, Ann.
   Meet my friend, José.
       Pleased to meet you, José.
   Meet my mother, Mrs. Naga.
       Pleased to meet you, Mrs. Naga.
   Meet my brother, Yukio.
       Pleased to meet you, Yukio.
   Meet my sister, Hiromi.
       Pleased to meet you, Hiromi.

Present Continuous
be + Verb + ing

Mike and Alice *are talking.*
They *are having* a party.
Hiromi and José *are coming.*
They *are studying* hard.
Who's *studying?* Mike and Alice *are studying.*
Who's *coming?* Hiromi and José *are coming.*
Who's *having* a party? They're *having* a party.

Practice
Numbers 0 (zero) to 20 (twenty)

0	zero	11	eleven
1	one	12	twelve
2	two	13	thirteen
3	three	14	fourteen
4	four	15	fifteen
5	five	16	sixteen
6	six	17	seventeen
7	seven	18	eighteen
8	eight	19	nineteen
9	nine	20	twenty
10	ten		

Telling Time

What time is it?
It's . . . . o'clock.

It's seven
o'clock.

It's five after
seven.
(7:05)

It's seven fifteen.
It's a quarter past seven.
(7:15)

It's seven thirty.
(7:30)

It's seven forty.
(Twenty minutes
till eight) (7:40)

It's seven forty-five.
(Fifteen till eight)

It's eight o'clock.
(8:00 AM or PM)

It's twelve mid-
night.

It's twelve noon.
(12:00 PM)

The Clock

I'm a clock.
I never stop.
Minute after minute,
hour after hour I go
tic-toc-tic-toc . . .

Counting

Counting / 20 to 0

twenty, nineteen, eighteen, seventeen, sixteen, fifteen, fourteen, thirteen, twelve, eleven, ten, nine, eight, seven, six, five, four, three, two, one, zero
20—19—18—17—16—15—14—13—12—11—10—9—8—7—6—
5—4—3—2—1—0

Counting / *odd* numbers

one, three, five, seven, nine, eleven, thirteen, fifteen, seventeen, nineteen
1—3—5—7—9—11—13 –15—17—19

Counting / *even* numbers

two, four, six, eight, ten, twelve, fourteen, sixteen, eighteen, twenty
2—4—6—8—10—12—14—16—18—20

Telling Time

What time is it? —————————————————————— 1:00

Write longhand ——————————————————————— 1:15

——————————————————————— 2:30

——————————————————————— 3:40

——————————————————————— 3:45

——————————————————————— 4:00

——————————————————————— 12:00 p.m.

——————————————————————— 12:00 a.m.

It's 7:00 a.m.	It's time to get up.
It's 7:15 a.m.	It's time to eat breakfast.
It's 8:00 a.m.	It's time for school.
It's 12:00 noon.	It's time for lunch.
It's 4:00 p.m.	It's time to go home.
It's 5:00 p.m.	It's time to study.
It's 7:00 p.m.	It's time to watch TV.
It's 10:00 p.m.	It's time to wash up.
It's 11:00 p.m.	It's time to sleep.

When?—early/late/on time

When is school out today?	School is out *early*.
Is Mike up *early*?	Yes, he's up *early*.
Do classes begin *early*?	Yes, they begin *early*.
Does Mike's ride come *early*?	It comes *early* sometimes.
Is the bus *on time* today?	Yes, it's *on time*.
	No, it's not on time. It's *late*.

Always/never

Is Hiromi *late* for class?	Hiromi's never *late*.
	She's always *on time*.
Does José come to school *early*?	José comes to school *early*.
	He's *never* late.
Is the bus *always* on time?	The bus is *never on time*.
	It's sometimes *early*;
	it's sometimes *late*.

Today

Alice: Mr. Powell is sick *today*.

Mike: He's *never* sick. He's only *late*.

Alice: No, *today* Mr. Powell's sick.

Mike: How do you know that?

Alice: I know because he's *never late* for class.

Mike: You're right, Alice. *Today* Mr. Powell's sick.

What Time Is It?

It's time to get up.
What time is it?
It's 7:00 a.m.

It's time to eat breakfast.
What time is it?
It's 7:15 a.m.

It's time for school.
What time is it?
It's 8:00 a.m.

It's time for lunch.
What time is it?
It's 12:00 noon.

It's time to go home.
What time is it?
It's 4:00 o'clock.

It's time to study.
What time is it?
It's 5:00 o'clock.

It's time to watch TV.
What time is it?
It's 7:00 p.m.

It's time to wash up.
What time is it?
It's 10:00 p.m.

It's time to sleep.
What time is it?
It's 11:00 p.m.

Tell What You Are Doing

It's 7:00 a.m.
  What are you doing now?
It's 7:15 a.m.
  What are you doing now?
It's 8:00 a.m.
  What are you doing now?

It's 12:00 noon.

What are you doing now?

It's 4 o'clock.

What are you doing now?

It's 5 o'clock.

What are you doing now?

It's 7:00 p.m.

What are you doing now?

It's 10:00 p.m.

What are you doing now?

It's 11:00 p.m.

What are you doing now?

Copy

it's __it's__ late __late__ It's late. __It's late.__
it's __it's__ early __early__ It's early. __It's early.__
time __time__ to __to__ get up __get up__
It's time to get up. __It's time to get up.__
for __for__ lunch __lunch__ to study __to study__
It's time to study. __It's time to study.__
watch __watch__ wash up __wash up__ sleep __sleep__
It's time to watch TV. __It's time to watch TV.__
It's time to wash up. __It's time to wash up.__
It's time to sleep. __It's time to sleep.__

Practice

Possessive Adjectives
my/your/his/her/our/their

This is *my* book.
Is this *your* book? Yes, it is. It's *my* book.

This is *his* sister.
Is that *your* sister? No, it isn't. It's *his* sister.

This is *her* car.
Is this *your* car? No, it isn't. It's *her* car.

That's *our* classroom.
Is this *their* classroom? No, it isn't. It's *our* classroom.

Present Continuous

1. Mike and Alice are talking.
   Who's talking?
   Mike and Alice *are talking.*

2. When are they talking?
   (at 7:00 a.m.)
   They're *talking* at seven o'clock.

3. Who's studying hard?
   (Hiromi and José)
   Hiromi and José *are studying* hard.

4. What are they studying?
   (history)
   They're *studying* history.

5. When are they eating breakfast?
   (at 7:45 a.m.)
   They're *eating* breakfast at a quarter to eight.

6. Who's coming to dinner?
   (Isaac and Victoria)
   Isaac and Victoria *are coming* to dinner.

7. Who's having a break?
   (Alice and Mike)
   Alice and Mike *are having* a break.

8. Who's coming late?
   (Mike's ride)
   Mike's ride *is coming* late.

9. Who's taking a bus?
   (Mike)
   Mike'*s taking* a bus.

Time Expressions
today/early/late/on time

1. What comes late today?
   (the bus)
   The bus comes *late today.*

2. What's not on time?
   (the ride)
   Mike's ride is *late.* It's not *on time.*

3. Why is school out early today?
   (Mr. Powell is sick.)
   School's out *early today* because Mr. Powell's sick.

4. When are they going to the movies?
   (today)
   They're going to the movies *today.*

5. Is Mike on time?
   (no)
   No, Mike's not *on time.*

always/never/sometimes

1. Does Mike get up early?
   (yes, always)
   Yes, Mike *always* gets up early.

2. Is Mr. Powell always sick?
   (no, not always)
   No, Mr. Powell is not *always* sick.

3. Does Hiromi watch TV?
   (no, never)
   No, Hiromi *never* watches TV.

4. Does the bus come on time?
   (sometimes)
   The bus *sometimes* comes on time.

5. Is Mike always late?
   (no, sometimes)
   No, he's *sometimes* late.

Substitution Drill

1. Mike and Alice are **talking**.
                       studying.
                       eating.

2. Hiromi and José are **happy**.
                       sad.
                       hungry.

3. **The bus** is late today.
   Pablo
   Alice

4. Pablo **gets up** at **seven** o'clock. (7:00)
        eats breakfast   **seven-fifteen** (7:15)
        lunch   **noon** (12:00)

5. Hiromi is **always** late.
        never
        sometimes

6. Is the bus always **late?**
                on time?
                early?

7. **You're** never late.
  I'm
  He's
  We're

8. She's **sometimes** early.
        never
        always

9. It's time for **breakfast.**
          lunch.
          dinner.

10. Are you **always** late?
        never
        sometimes

11. This is **my** book.
        his
        her

12. Is this **your** teacher?
        our
        their

13. Mr. Powell is **our** teacher.
       his
       her

14. What's **your** name?
      his
      her

15. Is that **his** newspaper?
      her
      our

16. This is my **doctor.**
      professor.
      TV repairman.
      lawyer.

17. That's his/her **waitress.**
      nurse.
      mechanic.

18. Is this your **father?**
      mother?
      sister?
      brother?

19. That's **his** sister.
      her
      my
      their

20. What's **your** name?
      his
      her
      my

21. Where's your **classroom?**
      book?
      pen?
      pencil?

Copy

one	*one*	six	*six*
two	*two*	seven	*seven*
three	*three*	eight	*eight*
four	*four*	nine	*nine*
five	*five*	ten	*ten*

eleven	*eleven*	sixteen	*sixteen*
twelve	*twelve*	seventeen	*seventeen*
thirteen	*thirteen*	eighteen	*eighteen*
fourteen	*fourteen*	nineteen	*nineteen*
fifteen	*fifteen*	twenty	*twenty*

Exercises

Write the numbers

Example: $1 + 2 = 3$ <u>*one* plus *two* = *three*</u>

$2 + 3 = 5$ _____ + _____ = _____

$3 + 4 = 7$ _____ + _____ = _____

$4 + 5 = 9$ _____ + _____ = _____

$5 + 6 = 11$ _____ + _____ = _____

$6 + 7 = 13$ _____ + _____ = _____

$7 + 8 = 15$ _____ + _____ = _____

$8 + 9 = 17$ _____ + _____ = _____

$9 + 10 = 19$ _____ + _____ = _____

$1 + 1 = 2$ _____ + _____ = _____

$2 + 2 = 4$ _____ + _____ = _____

$2 + 4 = 6$ _____ + _____ = _____

$2 + 6 = 8$ _____ + _____ = _____

$5 + 5 = 10$ _____ + _____ = _____

$7 + 5 = 12$ _____ + _____ = _____

$6 + 8 = 14$ _____ + _____ = _____

$10 + 6 = 16$ _____ + _____ = _____

$9 + 9 = 18$ _____ + _____ = _____

Fill in the Blanks

Fill in *my/your/his/her/our/their*

> **Example:** This is Ann. She's <u>my</u> friend.

I'm José Betancourt. _____ name is José.

You are Hiromi Naga. _____ name is Hiromi.

She is Ann Carson. _____ name is Ann.

He's Isaac Betancourt. _____ brother is José Betancourt.

We are Hiromi and Yukio. _____ parents are in Japan.

They are José and Victoria. _____ relatives live in Venezuela.

Fill in *Present continuous*

> **Examples:** Who's talking? (Hiromi and Ron)
> <u>Hiromi and Ron are talking.</u>
>
> What's Angel doing? (playing)
> <u>Angel's playing.</u>

Who's talking ? (Lisa) _____

Who's studying? (José and Ron) _____

Who's waiting? (Mike) _____

Who's going to the movies? (Alice and Mike) _____

_____

What's he doing? (studying) _____

What's Isaac doing? (playing soccer) _____

What's Victoria doing? (talking) _____

Guess the Time

> **Example:** Mike's getting up.
> What time is it?
> It's (7:00 a.m.) seven o'clock.

Mike's eating breakfast.
What time is it?
It's _____

Mike's in the classroom.
What time is it?
It's _____

Alice is eating lunch.
What time is it?
It's _____

Alice is waiting for the bus.
What time is it?
It's _____

Alice and Mike are studying.
What time is it?
It's _____

Alice and Mike are watching TV.
What time is it?
It's _____

Alice is washing up.
What time is it?
It's _____

Mike's sleeping.
What time is it?
It's _____

Fill in the Blanks
Fill in *today/early/late/on time*

> **Example:** When does the bus come today? (late)
> <u>The bus comes late today.</u>

When's Mike getting up? (early)

When's Alice coming to class? (on time)

_____

When are Alice and Mike sad? (today)

_____

When's school out today? (early)

_____

When's Mr. Powell sick? (today)

_____

When are they coming to dinner? (late)

_____

When's her ride here? (on time)

_____

Fill in *always/never/sometimes*

> **Example:** When's Mr. Powell sick? (sometimes)
> <u>Mr. Powell's sick sometimes.</u>

When's the bus late? (sometimes)

_____

When's Mike on time? (always)

_____

When's Alice watching TV? (sometimes)

_____

When's Mike late for class? (never)

_____

When are Mike and Alice going to the movies? (sometimes)

_____

Unscramble

Unscramble the letters to make words.

Example: ebrka = break

meti _____ aydot _____

swayla _____ veren _____

lyea _____ tlae _____

ryou _____ rhe _____

rou _____ htier _____

Answers to Unscramble:

time; always; early; your; our; today; never; late; her; their

Puzzle

We use all these words to make the PRESENT CONTINUOUS. They all end in *–ing*. First, fill in the word on the line, then write it in the puzzle on the following page.

1. Mike and Alice are _____ up early today.
    down

2. He's _____ a bus today.
    down

3. Mike's ride is _____ him up early.
    down

4. Alice asks: "What are you _____ tonight?"
    down

5. Mike and Alice are _____ during school break.
    across

6. Mike says: "How about _____ to the movies?"
    across

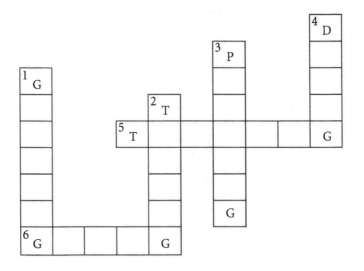

Change Questions to Statements

Change the following statements to *yes/no* questions.

Example: Mike and Alice are talking. = <u>Are Mike and Alice talking?</u>

Hiromi and José are studying. _____

Manuel and Angel are eating. _____

Victoria and Isaac are coming. _____

Hiromi and José are happy. _____

Mr. and Mrs. Naga are sad. _____

The Carsons are hungry. _____

Example: The bus is late. = <u>Is the bus late?</u>

Ann is on time. _____

Mike is late. _____

Ann is early. _____

Angel is never late. _____

Manuel is sometimes on time. _____

Helen is early today. _____

Example: This is his book. = <u>Is this his book?</u>

That's her doctor. _____

This is my mechanic. _____

That's my teacher. _____

This is our lawyer. _____

That's his father. _____

This is our daughter. _____

That's their cousin. _____

What Questions

Example: My name is Mike. = <u>What's your name?</u>

His name is Manuel. _____

It's time to get up. _____

Her brother's name is Yukio. _____

Our telephone number is 436-0152. _____

Their address is 122 Cherry Street. _____

Completion
Complete the reading using the words below.

sick   break   late   are   taking   early

Mike and Alice _____ talking during their break. School is out _____ today. Mr. Powell's _____ . Mike's _____ a bus. The bus is _____ .

Complete the talk using the words below.

What   How about   What time

Alice: _____ is it?

Mike: It's a quarter past three.

Alice: _____ are you doing tonight?

Mike: Oh, I don't know.

Alice: _____ a movie?

Mike: O.K. See you around seven o'clock.

Copy

early _early_   Mike's getting up early. _Mike's getting up early._

late _late_   Ann is never late. _Ann is never late._

sometimes _sometimes_   The bus is sometimes on time. _The bus is sometimes on time._

sleeping _sleeping_   Manuel is sleeping now. _Manuel is sleeping now._

eating _eating_   We're eating dinner. _We're eating dinner._

Exercises

Writing

Write a situation about the following dialogue.

Hiromi: Hello, Mom. How are you?

Mrs. Naga: Hi, Hiromi. I'm fine.

Hiromi: How's Father?

Mrs. Naga:	He is right here.
Mr. Naga:	Hello, Hiromi. It's nice talking to you.
Hiromi:	I'm happy, too.
Mr. Naga: Mrs. Naga:	Take care now.
Hiromi:	I will. Thanks for calling.
Mr. Naga: Mrs. Naga:	Good-bye.
Hiromi:	Good-bye.

Write a dialogue about the following situation.

You're driving a car.
Your friend is waiting at the bus stop.
You stop to give her a ride.
She thanks you.

Proverb

It's better late than never. (It's never too late to learn.)

CHAPTER FOUR

Dinner at the Carsons'

IN THIS CHAPTER

Possessive Pronouns: Question *whose?*
mine/yours/his/hers/ours/yours/theirs

Prepositions: *in/at/on/behind/to/by/under/inside*

Days in the week: *Monday/Tuesday/Wednesday/
Thursday/Friday/Saturday/Sunday*

One and *Many*—*Singular* and *Plural*

Ordinal Numbers: *first/second/third/etc.*

Read

Situation

Manuel Vargas and José Betancourt are invited to dinner at the Carsons'. Hiromi and Ann are helping with the preparations. Hiromi sets the table with six plates, spoons, forks, knives and napkins. Ann is making a cool drink. She sets six glasses on the table.

Hiromi is worried. There is not enough food for everybody. Suddenly the phone rings. It is José. He is doing homework, and he is not coming to dinner. The girls are sorry. But now there is enough food for everybody.

Listen/Talk

Dialogue

Hiromi: Well, everything's on the table.

Ann: Hmmm..not quite.

Hiromi: Is that so?

Ann:	I'm afraid there's not enough food.
Hiromi:	Not enough?
Ann:	There's only food for five.
Hiromi:	Let's run over to the grocery.
Ann:	You forget it's Sunday.
	(*Phone rings*)
Ann:	Hello?
José:	Hello, this is José.
Ann:	Hi, José. You're late.
José:	Sorry, I'm not coming.
Ann:	Really? Why's that?
José:	I'm doing my homework.
Ann:	I see. That's a good excuse.
José:	Thanks. See you on Monday.
Ann:	'Bye now.

Copy

invited ___*invited*___ to dinner ___*to dinner*___

invited to dinner ___*invited to dinner*___

They are invited to dinner. ___*They are invited to dinner.*___

plate ___*plate*___ spoon ___*spoon*___ fork ___*fork*___ knife ___*knife*___

plates ___*plates*___ spoons ___*spoons*___ forks ___*forks*___ knives ___*knives*___

glass ___*glass*___ glasses ___*glasses*___ napkin ___*napkin*___ napkins ___*napkins*___

on the table ___*on the table*___ worried ___*worried*___

the phone ___*the phone*___ rings ___*rings*___

The phone rings. ___*The phone rings.*___

sorry ___*sorry*___ the girls ___*the girls*___

The girls are sorry. ___*The girls are sorry.*___

Repeat

What Is It?

This is a table.
It's a table.

They're tables.

This is a spoon.
It's a spoon.

They're spoons.

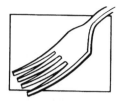

This is a fork.
It's a fork.

They're forks.

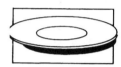

This is a plate.
It's a plate.

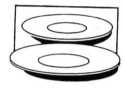

They're plates.

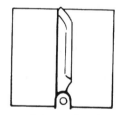

This is a knife.
It's a knife.

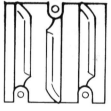

They're knives.

This is a napkin.
It's a napkin.

They're napkins.

They're glasses.

This is a glass.
It's a glass.

They're
phones.

This is a phone.
It's a phone.

What Are They Doing?

In the classroom . . . they study
   They study in the classroom.

In the dining room . . . they eat
   They eat in the dining room.

In the bedroom . . . they sleep
   They sleep in the bedroom.

In the bathroom . . . they wash up
   They wash up in the bathroom.

In the library . . . they read
   They read in the library.

In the lab . . . they listen
   They listen in the lab.

In the office . . . they talk
   They talk in the office.

In the dining room . . . they eat
   They eat in the dining room.

In the bedroom . . . they sleep
   They sleep in the bedroom.

In the bathroom . . . they wash up
   They wash up in the bathroom.

In the library . . . they read
   They read in the library.

In the lab . . . they listen
   They listen in the lab.

In the office . . . they talk
   They talk in the office.

Copy

classroom _classroom_   they study _they study_
They study in the classroom. _They study in the classroom._
dining room _dining room_   they eat _they eat_
They eat in the dining room. _They eat in the dining room._
sleep _sleep_   bedroom _bedroom_
They sleep in the bedroom. _They sleep in the bedroom._
bathroom _bathroom_   wash up _wash up_
They wash up in the bathroom. _They wash up in the bathroom._
library _library_   read _read_
They read in the library. _They read in the library._
lab _lab_   listen _listen_
They listen in the lab. _They listen in the lab._
office _office_   talk _talk_
They talk in the office. _They talk in the office._

Pronunciation Practice

Words

napkin	a napkin	napkins
kitchen	a kitchen	kitchens
table	a table	tables
spoon	a spoon	spoons
fork	a fork	forks
knife	a knife	knives
drink	a drink	drinks
glass	a glass	glasses

Questions

Is Manuel invited to dinner?

Is Hiromi helping with
  the preparations?

Does Hiromi set the table?

Does the phone ring?

Is it José?

Is José sick?

Is José coming to dinner?

Why isn't José coming?

Are the girls sorry?

Is there enough food?

Statements

Manuel and José are invited to dinner.

Hiromi and Ann are helping
  with the preparations.

Hiromi and Ann set the table.

Suddenly, the phone rings.

It's José.

José is not sick.

José isn't coming to dinner.

He is doing homework.

The girls are sorry.

There's enough food.

Questions

Who's invited to dinner?

Are they invited?

Who's helping?

Are they helping?

Is José coming to dinner?

Why isn't José coming?

Is Hiromi worried?

Why is Hiromi worried?

Answers

José and Manuel are invited.

Yes, they are.

Hiromi and Ann are helping.

Yes, they are.

No, he isn't.

José's doing his homework.

Yes, Hiromi is worried.

Yes, she is.

There is not (isn't) enough food.

Identify—What's Happening?

This is Hiromi.
She's setting
the table.

That's Ann.
She's also setting
the table.

The table is set.
There are six *plates* on the table.

spoons
forks
knives
glasses
napkins

What's José doing?
José's calling Ann.
Why's José calling?
José's doing his homework.

What's Ann doing?
Ann's making a cool drink.
She's making a drink for dinner.

What are they doing?
They're eating dinner.
How many persons are at the table?
There are five (5) persons at the table.

Study

Possessive Pronouns
Whose—mine/yours/his/hers/ours/theirs

Whose book is this?
  It's my book. It's *mine.*
Whose notebook is that? Is it yours?
  No, it isn't. It's *his.*
Whose classroom is this? It's our classroom.
  It's *ours.*
Whose cafeteria is that? It's their cafeteria.
  It's *theirs.*

Hiromi: That's Mr. Powell's history class, isn't it?
José: Yes, it is.
Hiromi: Is Mr. Powell absent today?
José: Yes, he is. He's in bed sick.

Prepositions
in/at/on/behind/to/by/under

Where is Mr. Powell?
  He's in *his* office.

Where's he sitting?
  He's sitting *at* his desk.

What's *under* the chair?
  There's a book *under* the chair.

What's *on* his chair?
  His glasses are *on* his chair.

What's *behind* the desk?
  There's a chair *behind* the desk.

Where are you going?
  We're invited *to* dinner.

Where's Yukio sitting?
  He's sitting *on* a bench.

Where are they sitting?
  They're sitting *at* the table.

Who's he talking to?
  He's talking *to* a friend.

When will I see you?
  See you *at* seven o'clock.
  Well, it's good to see you!

We're here *on* time, aren't we?
Yes, of course. Where's José?
He's *behind in* his homework.
You mean, he isn't coming *to* dinner?
Sorry, he isn't. He's eating *at* the dorm.

Days in the Week

There are seven days in a week. We have school on Monday, Tuesday, Wednesday, Thursday and Friday. Monday is the first school day of the week. Friday is the last school day of the week. We have no school on Saturday and Sunday. We call Saturday and Sunday "weekend."

Repeat

Monday		*first* day of the week.
Tuesday		*second*
Wednesday		*third*
Thursday	is the	*fourth* day of the week.
Friday		*fifth*
Saturday		*sixth*
Sunday		*seventh*

Copy

one	— Monday is the first	*one*	*Monday is the first*
two	— Tuesday is second	*two*	*Tuesday is second*
three	— Wednesday is third	*three*	*Wednesday is third*
four	— Thursday is fourth	*four*	*Thursday is fourth*
five	— Friday is fifth	*five*	*Friday is fifth*
six	— Saturday is sixth	*six*	*Saturday is sixth*
seven	— Sunday is seventh	*seven*	*Sunday is seventh*
eight	— eighth	*eight*	*eighth*
nine	— ninth	*nine*	*ninth*
ten	— tenth	*ten*	*tenth*
eleven	— eleventh	*eleven*	*eleventh*
twelve	— twelfth	*twelve*	*twelfth*
thirteen	— thirteenth	*thirteen*	*thirteenth*
twenty	— twentieth	*twenty*	*twentieth*

Practice

One/Many (Singular/Plural)

Hiromi is *a student.*
 Hiromi and José *are students.*

Mr. Carson is *a lawyer.*
 There *are many lawyers* in town.

Mrs. Carson is *a doctor.*
 How *many doctors* do you know?

Hiromi is *a guest* of the Carsons.
 There *are guests* at the party.

José has *one* sister.

    Yukio has *two* sisters.

Mike is *a nurse.*

    There *are nurses* at the hospital.

Lisa is *a plumber.*

    In Lisa's family there *are three plumbers.*

Change to Many

Examples: She's a doctor.   = They're doctors.

                   He's a plumber.   = They're plumbers.

He's a student. = _____

He's a professor. = _____

He's a lawyer.   = _____

She's a nurse.   = _____

It's a classroom. = _____

It's a book.   = _____

It's a teacher.   = _____

It's a chair.   = _____

Change to One

Examples: They're friends. = It's a friend.

                   They're sisters. = She's a sister.

They're brothers. = _____

They're phones. = _____

They're spoons. = _____

They're forks.   = _____

They're tables.   = _____

They're napkins. = _____

They're drinks.   = _____

They're towns.   = _____

They're labs.   = _____

They're kitchens. = _____

Possessive Pronouns

1. There's a book on the desk.
   Is it José's (Hiromi's) book?
   No, it's not José's. It's Ann's (Mike's).
   Whose desk is that?
   Is it *Ann's*?
   No, it's *mine*.

2. Is this Dr. Carson's office?
   No, it's Mr. Powell's.
   Are you sure?
   Yes, I am. It's Mr. Powell's.

3. There's a notebook *on* the floor.
   Where is it?
   Over there, *behind* the door.
   Oh, that one.
   Whose is it?
   It's Ann's.

4. Look! There's a bench at the bus stop.
   Mike's sitting on it. Isn't he?
   It isn't Mike. It's Mike's friend, Angel.
   Oh, so it is! That's Mike behind Angel.

Counting

Odd *Numbers*

first (1st)   eleventh (11th)
third (3rd)   thirteenth (13th)
fifth (5th)   fifteenth (15th)
seventh (7th)   seventeenth (17th)
ninth (9th)   nineteenth (19th)

Even *Numbers*

second (2nd)   twelfth (12th)
fourth (4th)   fourteenth (14th)
sixth (6th)   sixteenth (16th)
eighth (8th)   eighteenth (18th)
tenth (10th)

Answer the Questions

> **Example:** Where's the English class? (8th floor)
> The English class is on the eighth floor.

Where's Doctor Carson's office? (15th floor)

_____

Where's the cafeteria? (12th floor)

_____

Where's the lab? (14th floor)

_____

Where's your class? (17th floor)

_____

Where's the garage? (19th street)

_____

Example: This is Monday. What day of the week is it?
(1st) <u>Monday is the first day of the week.</u>

This is Tuesday. What day of the week is it?

(2nd) _____

This is Wednesday. What day of the week is it?

(3rd) _____

This is Thursday. What day of the week is it?

(4th) _____

This is Friday. What day of the week is it?

(5th) _____

This is Saturday. What day of the week is it?

(6th) _____

This is Sunday. What day of the week is it?

(7th) _____

Substitution Drill

1. Whose **book** is this?
      notebook
      desk
      chair

2. This is **my** book. It's **mine.**
         your   **yours.**
         her   **hers.**
         their   **theirs.**

3. Whose **notebook** is this? Is it **José's?**
         fork   **mine?**
         glass   **hers?**
         desk   **Mr. Powell's?**
         drink   **Ann's?**

4. No, it isn't **José's.**   I think it's **Hiromi's.**
      mine.   **Ann's.**
      hers.   **yours.**
      Mr. Powell's.   **Mr. Carson's.**

Practice

Write and Answer yes/no

    Example: Is that his mother?   <u>Yes, it is his mother.</u>
                                                      <u>No, it isn't his mother.</u>

Is that Ann's desk?   _____

Is this his book?   _____

Is that their room?   _____

Is that her notebook?   _____

Is that your pen?   _____

Is this your pen?   _____

Write and Ask yes/no *Question*

    Example: That's her brother.   <u>Is that her brother?</u>
                                                      <u>Isn't that her brother?</u>

This is Hiromi's book.   _____

This is his desk. _____

_____

That's their room. _____

_____

This is her notebook. _____

_____

That's our pen. _____

_____

This is my pencil. _____

_____

Listen and Write (Dictation)

first _____ day _____ week _____

Monday is the first day of the week. _____

office _____ second _____ floor _____

The office is on the second floor. _____

lab _____ fifth _____ floor _____

The lab is on the fifth floor. _____

Singular to Plural (one to many)

Examples: What is she?   What is he?
                 She's a doctor.   He's a lawyer.

                 What are they?   What are they?
                 They're doctors.   They're lawyers.

1. What is he?   2. What is she?
   He's a mechanic.   She is a nurse.

   _____   _____

   _____   _____

3. What is he?
   He's a student.

   _____

   _____

4. What is it?
   It's a car.

   _____

   _____

5. What is it?
   It's a table.

   _____

   _____

6. What is he?
   He's a professor.

   _____

   _____

7. What is she?
   She's a teacher.

   _____

   _____

8. What is it?
   It's a drink.

   _____

   _____

Plural to Singular (many *to* one)

Examples:

What are they?
They're teachers.

What is he?
He's a teacher.

What are they?
They're tables.

What is it?
It's a table?

1. What are they?
   They are doctors.

   _____

   _____

2. What are they?
   They're students.

   _____

   _____

3. What are they?
   They're plumbers.

   _____

   _____

4. What are they?
   They're lawyers.

   _____

   _____

5. What are they?
They're books.

_____

_____

6. What are they?
They're pencils.

_____

_____

7. What are they?
They're pens.

_____

_____

8. What are they?
They're forks.

_____

_____

Possessive Pronouns
mine/yours/his/hers/ours/theirs/'s

Examples: It's your book, isn't it? (no, Pablo's)
<u>No, it isn't. It's Pablo's.</u>

It's your TV, isn't it? (no, hers)
<u>No, it isn't. It's hers.</u>

1. It's your spoon, isn't it? (yes, mine)

_____

2. It's their classroom, isn't it? (yes, theirs)

_____

3. They're his books, aren't they? (no, mine)

_____

4. They're her friends, aren't they? (yes, hers)

_____

5. It's Hiromi's pencil, isn't it? (no, Yukio's)

_____

6. They're our desks, aren't they? (yes, ours)

_____

7. It's Ann's pen, isn't it? (yes, hers)

_____

Prepositions
in/at/on/to/behind/under

> **Example:** Is the book *on* the desk? (no, under)
> No, the book is *under* the desk.

1. Is the notebook behind the chair? (no, on)

_____

2. Is Ann in her room? (no, library)

_____

3. Are Hiromi's friends at the party? (yes)

_____

4. Are Hiromi's parents in the U.S.A.? (no, Japan)

_____

5. Are the plates under the table? (no, on)

_____

6. Are the books behind the door? (no, on the table)

_____

7. Where's Mr. Carson? (in his office)

_____

8. Where is the chair? (behind, desk)

_____

9. Where's Hiromi's notebook? (on the floor)

_____

10. Is the chair behind the door? (no, in the room)

_____

Days of the Week
weekdays/first/second, etc.

> **Example:** Monday's the third day of the week, isn't it? (no, 1st)
> No, it isn't. It's the first day.

1. Tuesday is the first day of the week, isn't it? (no, 2nd)

_____

2. Thursday is the third day of the week, isn't it? (no, 4th)

_____

3. Saturday is the fifth day of the week, isn't it? (no, 6th)

_____

4. Sunday is the seventh day of the week, isn't it? (yes)

_____

5. Friday is the third day of the week, isn't it? (no, 5th)

_____

6. Wednesday is the second day of the week, isn't it? (no, 3rd)

_____

Completion
Complete the dialogue. Use the words below.

Monday   second   Saturday

It's _____ , the first day of the week.

Which day comes _____ ? It's Tuesday.

I always go to the movies on _____ .

I know, it's the sixth day of the week.

whose   hers   yours

_____ book is this?

Is it _____ ?

Yes, it's mine.

Is this book Ann's?

Yes, it is. It's _____ .

Fill in the Blanks

Fill in the correct word. Use the words below.

there   behind   in   offices

Where's Mr. Powell?

He's _____ his office.

Is that _____ the cafeteria?

I guess it is. There are many _____ there.

Thank you.

You're welcome.

Repeat—Who Is Who

Who's this?
This is Hiromi.
Whose sister is she?
She's Yukio's sister.

Who's this?
This is Yukio.
Whose brother is he?
He's Hiromi's brother.

Who's this?
It's Mr. Carson.
He's Ann's father.

Who's that?
That's Mrs. Carson.
She's Ann's mother.

Who's this?
This is Jane.
Who's she?
Whose sister is she?
She's Yukio's and Hiromi's sister.

Who's that?
That's Manuel Vargas.
Whose secretary is he?
He's Mr. Carson's secretary.

Who's that?
That's Mr. Powell.
Whose teacher is he?
He's Hiromi's teacher.

Who's this?
This is Mrs. Powell.
Whose wife is she?
She's Mr. Powell's wife.

Who's that?
That's Ann Carson.
Whose friend is she?
She's José's friend.

Who's this?
This is Isaac Betancourt.
Whose brother is he?
He's José's and Victoria's brother.

Who's that?
That's Donald Powell.
He's Ann's brother and
Mr. and Mrs. Powell's son.

Who are they?
They're Mr. and Mrs.
Naga. They're
Hiromi's, Yukio's
and Jane's parents.

Who are they?
They're Mr. and Mrs.
Betancourt. They're
José's parents. They're
also Isaac's and
Victoria's parents.

Exercises

Sentences With Possessives

Make a sentence with the *possessive/'s.*

> **Example:** This is Yukio Naga.
>
> Whose brother is Yukio? (Hiromi)
>
> <u>Yukio is Hiromi's brother.</u>

1. This is Ann Carson.

    Whose daughter is she? (Mr. Carson)

    _____

2. This is a desk.

    Whose desk is it? (Mr. Powell)

    _____

3. This is a pencil.

    Whose pencil is it? (Manuel)

    _____

4. This is a book.

    Whose book is it? (Victoria)

    _____

5. This is Angel Lopez.

    Whose friend is he? (Donald)

    _____

mine/yours/his/hers/ours/theirs

> **Examples:** This is a pen.   This is a book.
>
> Whose pen is it? (you)   Whose book is it? (they)
>
> <u>It is yours.</u>   <u>It is theirs.</u>

1. There's a desk.

   Whose is it? (I)

   _____

2. That's a pencil.

   Whose is it? (you)

   _____

3. This is a notebook.

   Whose is it? (he)

   _____

4. They are pens.

   Whose are they? (she)

   _____

5. They're spoons.

   Whose are they? (we)

   _____

6. They're glasses.

   Whose are they? (you)

   _____

7. They are forks.

   Whose are they? (they)

   _____

Completion

Complete the dialogue using the words below.

in   on   at   that's

Mike: What's _____ the second floor?

Angel: _____ my English class.

Mike: Is Mr. Powell _____ his office now?

Angel: No, he's there _____ 9 o'clock.

Unscramble

Unscramble the letters to make words.

Example: ntwo = <u>town</u>

tse _____ pleh _____

fodo _____ gnir _____

rmod _____ rofk _____

ersu _____ sdek _____

olorf _____ slasc _____

Answers to Unscramble:

set; help; food; ring; fork; dorm; desk; sure; floor; class

Change Statements to Questions

Change the following statements to appropriate questions.

Example: This is Mike's book.—<u>Whose book is this?</u>

1. This is Ann's English class.   _____

2. This is Mrs. Powell's garage.   _____

3. This is Angel's TV repair shop.   _____

4. That's José's ride.   _____

5. That's Hiromi's teacher.   _____

Example: The fork is on the table.—<u>Where is the fork?</u>

1. The plate is under the chair.   _____

2. The students are in the classroom.   _____

3. Ann is at the door.   _____

4. Mike's behind the desk.   _____

5. Hiromi's going to class.   _____

Puzzle

This PUZZLE tells about the things you *do* and prepare when you *invite* a friend to your home for dinner.

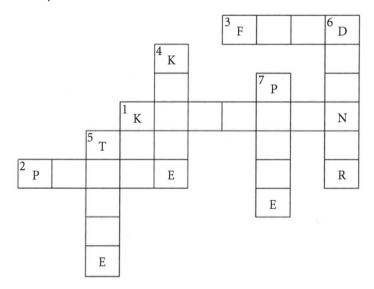

Across

1. The place where you cook the food.
2. You put your food on it.
3. You eat it.

Down

4. You cut the meat with it.
5. You put plates, spoons, etc. on it.
6. You invite your friend to have it with you.
7. You call up your friend on it.

Fill in the Blanks

Complete the reading using the words below.

rings   sets   are   to   making

Manuel and José _____ invited _____ dinner.
Hiromi _____ the table. Ann's _____ a cold drink.
Suddenly, the phone _____ .

Complete the talk using the words below.

Sunday   to   there's   that   on

Hiromi: Well, everything's _____ the table.

Ann: Hmm ... not quite.

Hiromi: Is _____ so?

Ann: I'm afraid _____ not enough food.

Hiromi: Let's run over _____ the grocery.

Ann: You forget it's _____ .

Listen and Write

invited _____ invited to dinner _____

Manuel and Mike are invited to dinner. _____

makes _____ cool _____ drink _____

Ann makes a cool drink. _____

desk _____ door _____ on _____ behind _____

The book is on the desk. _____

The desk is behind the door. _____

Write a situation about the following dialogue.

Ann: You're coming to dinner, aren't you?

José: Sorry, I'm doing my homework.

Ann: That's O.K. See you on Monday.

José: It's on Tuesday. On Monday there are no classes.

Ann: Oops, I forgot. It's a holiday.

Write a dialogue about the following situation.

You ask for your English classroom.
Someone tells you it's on the seventh floor.
You ask for the building.
Someone says it's the library building.

Proverb

First things first. (Doing one thing at a time.)

CHAPTER FIVE

A Trip to the Zoo

IN THIS CHAPTER

Command and Polite Request:
would you . . ?/ shall we . . ?/ let's . . .

Demonstratives: *these/those*

Adjectives = Words that Describe

Use of *where/tag question*

The Seasons: Spring/Summer/Fall/Winter

Months: *January/February/March/April/*
May/June/July/August/September/
October/November/December

Object Pronouns

Read

Situation

We are in a big zoo. The zoo is in San Diego, California. The zoo is beautiful. There are many animals in the zoo. It is interesting to visit a zoo. It is summer, and there is no school. June, July, and August are vacation months.

Listen/Talk

Dialogue

Part One

Mr. Powell:	Open your books to page thirty-nine.
Hiromi:	Look, it's a picture of a zoo.
Mr. Powell:	Please read the names of the animals.
Hiromi:	There's a lion and a camel . . .

José:	. . . and here's a tiger and a monkey . . .
Ann:	. . . and a big bear.
Mr. Powell:	O.K. Close your books. Now tell what you know about the animals.

Part Two

Mr. Powell:	Come in, Mike. Close the door.
Mike:	Good morning, Mr. Powell.
Mr. Powell:	Good morning, Mike.
Mike:	What's our lesson for tomorrow?
Mr. Powell:	Study the animals in a zoo.
Mike:	That's all?
Mr. Powell:	Yes, that's all.
Mike:	That's wonderful. I know them already.

Copy

zoo _zoo_   interesting _interesting_

The zoo is interesting. _The zoo is interesting._

beautiful ___*beautiful*___ The zoo is beautiful. ___*The zoo is beautiful.*___

animals ___*animals*___ There are many animals. ___*There are many animals.*___

visit ___*visit*___ We visit the zoo. ___*We visit the zoo.*___

Repeat—Who?—What?

Who's that?
That's Mr. Powell.

What's that?
That's a tiger.

Who's this?
This is Mike.

What's this?
This is a bear.

What's this?
This is a lion.

What's this?
This is a monkey.

What's that?
That's a camel.

What's that?
That's a wolf.

What's that?
That's an elephant.

What's this?
This is a cat.

What's this?
This is a giraffe.

What's that?
That's a dog.

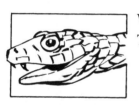

What's this?
This is a snake.

What's this?
This is a horse.

What's that?
That's a gorilla.

What's that?
That's a cow.

Extra Dialogue

Angel: Where are you going, Mike?
Mike: Why, to the zoo, my friend.
Angel: What's your business there?
Mike: I'm feeding the animals, that's what!

Answer the Questions

1. Where is Mike going?
2. What's Mike's business there?
3. Who's asking the questions?

Copy

there's _there's_____ lion _lion_____ in zoo _in zoo_____
There's a lion in the zoo. _There's a lion in the zoo._____
feeding _feeding_____ the animals _the animals_____
Mike's feeding the animals. _Mike's feeding the animals._____
elephant _elephant_____ big _big_____ animal _animal_____
The elephant is a big animal. _The elephant is a big animal._____

Pronunciation Practice

Words

an animal	the animal	animals
an elephant	the elephant	elephants
a tiger	the tiger	tigers
a monkey	the monkey	monkeys
interesting	beautiful	big
vacation	spring	summer
fall	autumn	winter

Questions

Where are we?
Where's the zoo?
Is the zoo beautiful?
Where are the animals?
Is the zoo interesting?
Why do we visit the zoo?
What three months are
    vacation months?

Statements

We're in a big zoo.
The zoo is in San Diego.
The zoo's beautiful.
The animals are in the zoo.
The zoo's interesting.
It's summer, and there's no school.
June, July, and August are
    vacation months.

Questions	*Answers/yes/no*
Are we in the zoo?	Yes, we're in the zoo.
We're in the zoo, aren't we?	Yes, we are.
Are we in a zoo?	No, we aren't.
Is the zoo in San Diego?	Yes, it is.
The zoo is in San Diego, isn't it?	Yes, it's in San Diego.
Is the zoo beautiful?	Yes, the zoo is beautiful.
The zoo is beautiful, isn't it?	Yes, it is.
There are few animals in the zoo, aren't there?	No, there are many animals in the zoo.
Isn't it interesting to visit the zoo?	Yes, it is. It's interesting.
Aren't April and May vacation months?	No, they aren't.

Command and *Polite Request*

Commands
Come in. / Don't come in.
Sit down. / Don't sit down.
Open the door. / Don't open the door.
Open your books. / Don't open your books.
Close your books. / Don't close your books.

Polite Requests
Listen, please. / Please listen.
Come in, please. / Please don't come in.
Please come in.
Open the door, please. / Please don't open the door.
Please open the door.
Open your books, please. / Please don't open the books.
Please open your books.

Would you . . .?
Would you come in, please?
Would you open the door, please?
Would you open the window, please?

Shall we . . . ?
Shall we sing now?
Shall we begin now?

Let's . . .
Let's read the lesson.
Let's practice some more.
Let's begin.

Study

Demonstratives: these/those
This is my sister, Hiromi.
These are my sisters, Hiromi and Jane.

That is my fork.
Those are my forks.

This pencil is mine.
These pencils are mine.

That book is hers.
Those books are theirs.

This is my friend, Ann.
These are my friends, Ann and Donald.

That's my dog, Fido.
Those are my dogs, Fido and Snappy.

Whose is this pen?—This pen is Mike's.
Whose are *these* pens?—*These* pens are ours.

Whose is that notebook?—That notebook is mine.
Whose are *those* notebooks?—*Those* notebooks are ours.

Adjectives: Words That Describe

ADJECTIVES tell us (1) *what kind,* (2) *how many,* or (3) *which one.* They come *before* the noun or *after* the verb *be.*

Who's a *good* student?	Hiromi's a *good* student.
	Hiromi and José are *good* students.
Who's that?	That's my *good* friend, José.
This is a zoo.	It's a *big* zoo.
What kind of a zoo is it?	It's a *big* zoo.
Those are horses.	Are they *beautiful?*
	Yes, they're *beautiful* horses.
Whose book is that?	It's mine. It's my *new* book.
	They're my *new* books.
What is this?—It's a zoo.	Is it *interesting?* Yes, it is.
Is it *big?*	Yes, the zoo is *big.*
How is Mrs. Naga?	Mrs. Naga is *sick.*
Is Mr. Naga *sick?*	No, Mr. Naga isn't *sick.* But he is *old.*
How old is Mrs. Betancourt?	Mrs. Betancourt is *young.*
Is this a *good* clock?	Yes, it is *good.* But sometimes the clock is *slow.*
How many chairs are there in the room?	There are *fourteen* chairs in the room.
In which row do you sit in class?	I sit in the *second* row.
Which day of the week is this?	This is the *fourth* day of the week.

Use of **where**

Where are you going?	I'm going to the zoo.
Where do you come from?	I come from Japan.
Where is Manuel from?	Manuel is from Argentina.
Where are your brothers?	They're at home.

Use of **Tag Question**

It's a beautiful zoo, isn't it?	Yes, it is.
That's an interesting book, isn't it?	No, it isn't.

He's a good teacher, isn't he?   Yes, he is.

She's an excellent doctor,   Yes, she is.
   isn't she?

They're good students,   Yes, they are.
   aren't they?

There are many animals in the   Yes, there are.
   zoo, aren't there?   No, there aren't.

The Seasons

There are four (4) SEASONS in a year:

SPRING   SUMMER   FALL (Autumn)   WINTER

1. *SPRING* is the season for planting things.

2. Everything grows during the *SUMMER*. It is hot during summer months.

3. *FALL* (Autumn) is harvest time.

4. *WINTER* is the cold season. People enjoy winter sports.

Numbers: *21 (twenty-one) to 100 (one hundred)*

21	twenty-one	60	sixty
22	twenty-two	61	sixty-one, etc.
30	thirty	70	seventy
31	thirty-one, etc.	71	seventy-one, etc.
40	forty	80	eighty
41	forty-one, etc.	81	eighty-one, etc.
50	fifty	91	ninety-one, etc.
51	fifty-one, etc.	100	one hundred

Counting: each tenth *number*

ten, twenty, thirty, forty, fifty, sixty, seventy, eighty, ninety, one hundred
10—20—30—40—50—60—70—80—90—100

Dates of the Seasons

Spring usually begins on the twentieth (20th) of March. It usually ends on the twentieth (20th) of June.

Summer usually begins on the twenty-first (21st) of June. It usually ends on the twenty-first (21st) of September.

Fall usually begins on the twenty-second (22nd) of September. It usually ends on the twentieth (20th) of December.

Winter usually begins on the twenty-first (21st) of December. It usually ends on the nineteenth (19th) of March.

Months

There are twelve (12) months in a year. There are four seasons in a year. Each season has three (3) months.

January (31 days) is the *first* (1st) month of the year.
February (28-29 days) is the *second* (2nd) month of the year.
March (31 days) is the *third* (3rd) month of the year.
April (30 days) is the *fourth* (4th) month of the year.
May (31 days) is the *fifth* (5th) month of the year.
June (30 days) is the *sixth* (6th) month of the year.
July (31 days) is the *seventh* (7th) month of the year.
August (31 days) is the *eighth* (8th) month of the year.
September (30 days) is the *ninth* (9th) month of the year.
October (31 days) is the *tenth* (10th) month of the year.
November (30 days) is the *eleventh* (11th) month of the year.
December (31 days) is the *twelfth* (12th) month of the year.

Use of Object Pronouns

Give the book to Ann.   Give it to *her.*
                              Give *her* the book.

Show the pen to Hiromi.

Show it to *her*.
Show *her* the pen.

Take this pencil to Mike.
It is my pen.
It is his book.
It is her notebook.
Is it your car?
Is this their class?
This isn't my book.
That's their class.
I'm sorry.
My dog is beautiful.
This lesson is easy.
That's my pencil.
No, it's mine.

Take it to *him*.
Give it to *me*.
Give it to *him*.
Show it to *her*.
Show it to *me*.
Take *me* there.
Give it to *her*.
Take *us* there.
Excuse *me*, please.
Please, show *him* to *me*.
Show it to *her*.
Give it to *me*.
Then show it to *me*.

Copy

spring __*spring*__ season __*season*__ first __*first*__

Spring is the first season. __*Spring is the first season.*__

summer __*summer*__ hot __*hot*__ Summer is hot. __*Summer is hot.*__

fall __*fall*__ gather __*gather*__ harvest __*harvest*__

Fall is harvest time. __*Fall is harvest time.*__

winter __*winter*__ cold __*cold*__ Winter is cold. __*Winter is cold.*__

AUGUST

Sunday	Monday	Tuesday	Wednesday	Thursday	Friday	Saturday
			1 English test	2	3	4 tennis 9-11
5 Lunch with Hiromi	6 see Mr. Powell	7	8 Lunch with Manuel	9	10 summer final exam	11 tennis 9-11
12 vacation begins	13 Mexico City	14	15	16	17	18
19	20	21	22 return home	23 buying school supplies	24	25 tennis 9-11
26 meeting new friends	27 registration	28 registration	29 begin Fall semester	30 meet Mr. Powell	31 lunch with Victoria	

Answer the Questions

1. When does José have an English test?
2. What does José do on Sunday the fifth of August?
3. When does José play tennis?
4. When does José have lunch with Manuel?
5. On what day are the summer finals?
6. When does José's vacation begin?
7. How long is José in Mexico?
8. When does José return home?
9. What does José do on August 26th?
10. When does the fall semester begin?
11. What does José do on August 31st?

Practice

Command/Polite Request

Example: Open the book. (would, please)
<u>Would you open the book, please?</u>

1. Close the door. (would, please)

_____

2. Stand up. (would, please)

_____

3. Sit down. (shall, now)

_____

4. Go to your room. (would, please)

_____

5. Come to my office. (would, please)

_____

6. Practice the dialogue. (let's)

_____

7. Read the lesson. (shall, now)

_____

8. Come in. (please)

_____

9. Pick up your book. (would, please)

_____

10. Eat your dinner. (would, please)

_____

Example: Sit down. (don't) = <u>Don't sit down.</u>

1. Read your lesson. (don't)

_____

2. Stand up. (don't)

_____

3. Open your books. (don't)

_____

4. Look at me. (don't)

_____

5. Feed the cat. (don't)

_____

6. Play with the dog. (don't)

_____

7. Come in. (don't)

_____

8. Go to your room. (don't)

_____

9. Close your door. (don't)

_____

10. Open the window. (don't)

_____

Substitution Drill

1. **Hiromi's** a good student.
   Ann's
   Manuel's
   Mike's

2. The **elephant** is a big animal.
   tiger
   lion
   camel

3. The zoo is **beautiful.**
   big.
   interesting.

4. That's a beautiful **book.**
   dog.
   pen.

5. This **dog** is sick.
    lion
    horse
    animal

1. **Come in**, please.
  Stand up,
  Sit down,

2. Close the **window**.
        door.
        books.

3. Please, **read your lesson**.
        go to your classroom.
        open the door.

4. Shall we **sit down** now?
        read
        go to class
        talk

5. **Look at me**, please.
  Feed the cat,
  Practice the dialogue,
  Come in,

Extra Dialogue

Helen: Isn't this tiger beautiful?
José: Yes, he is.
Alice: Let's see the lion over there.
Helen: Look, there's Hiromi.
José: It sure is.
Alice: You meet many friends in the zoo.

Practice

Adjectives

> ***Example:*** This is a book. (interesting)
> <u>This is an interesting book.</u>

1. This is a room. (small)

_____

2. That's a dog. (big)

_____

3. That's a tiger. (beautiful)

_____

4. That's my friend. (good)

_____

5. This is a zoo. (interesting)

_____

Months

> ***Example:*** It's January. Which month of the year is it? (1st)
> <u>January is the first (1st) month of the year.</u>

1. It's April. Which month of the year is it? (4th)

_____

2. It's September. Which month of the year is it? (9th)

_____

3. It's June. Which month of the year is it? (6th)

_____

4. It's November. Which month of the year is it? (11th)

_____

5. It's August. Which month of the year is it? (8th)

_____

6. It's March. Which month of the year is it? (3rd)

_____

7. It's December. Which month of the year is it? (12th)

_____

8. It's July. Which month of the year is it? (7th)

_____

9. It's October. Which month of the year is it? (10th)

_____

10. It's February. Which month of the year is it? (2nd)

_____

11. It's May. Which month of the year is it? (5th)

_____

Example: It's May now. How many days are there in May? (31)
<u>There are thirty-one days in May.</u>

1. It's December now. How many days are there? (31)

_____

2. It's February now. How many days are there in February? (28 or 29)

_____

3. It's September now. How many days are there in September? (30)

_____

4. It's November now. How many days are there in November? (30)

_____

5. It's June now. How many days are there in June? (30)

_____

Example: Today is June 15th. How many days until July? (15)
<u>There are fifteen (15) days until July.</u>

1. Today is August 10th. How many days until September? (21)

_____

2. Today is March 5th. How many days until April? (26)

_____

3. Today is July 11th. How many days until August? (20)

_____

4. Today is January 19th. How many days until February? (12)

_____

5. Today is October 23rd. How many days until November? (8)

_____

Example: It's the 16th of March. How many days until Spring? (5)
<u>There are five days until Spring.</u>

1. It's the 18th of March. How many days until Spring? (2)

_____

2. It's the 10th of June. How many days until Summer? (11)

_____

3. It's the 15th of September. How many days until Fall? (7)

_____

4. It's the 18th of December. How many days until Winter? (3)

_____

5. It's the 13th of March. How many days until the end of Winter? (6)

_____

Example: When is the Spring season? (March 22nd until June 21st)
<u>The Spring season is March 22nd until June 21st.</u>

1. When is the Summer season? (June 21st until September 22nd)

_____

2. When is the Fall season? (September 22nd until December 21st)

_____

3. When is the Winter season? (December 21st until March 21st)

_____

4. When does Spring begin? (March 21st)

_____

5. When does Summer begin? (June 21st)

_____

Object Pronouns

> **Example:** Give Mike the notebook. (it, him)
> Give <u>it</u> to <u>him</u>.

1. Send this letter to Ann. (it, her)

_____

2. Take this tape recorder to Mr. Powell. (it, him)

_____

3. Give the book to Manuel. (it, him)

_____

4. Show your jacket to Angel. (it, him)

_____

5. Show your car to Mrs. Carson. (it, her)

_____

Where *Questions*

> **Example:** There's Hiromi. <u>Where's Hiromi?</u>

1. Look! There's a lion! _____

2. We're going to class now. _____

3. A horse is in the street. _____

4. The tiger's in a cage. _____

5. Mr. Powell's in his office. _____

Substitution Drill

1. Isn't is a beautiful **day?**
             zoo?
             cat?
             book?

2. It's a beautiful **day**, isn't it?
             morning,
             evening,

3. It's an **interesting** zoo, isn't it?
         big
         beautiful

4. Isn't it cold in **January?**
             February?
             March?
             December?

5. It's hot in **May**, isn't it?
             June,
             July,
             August,

Identify

Guess What?

What's this?

It's _____ .

What's that?

That's ———————————— .

What's this?

It's ———————————— .

What's that?

That's ———————————— .

What's this?

It's ———————————— .

What's that?

That's ———————————— .

What's this?

It's _____.

What's that?

That's _____.

What's this?

It's _____.

What's that?

That's _____.

What's this?

It's _____.

What's that?

That's _____.

What's this?

It's _____.

What's that?

That's _____.

Write

Example: What's that? (big, elephant)

<u>That's a big elephant.</u>

1. What's this? (interesting, book)

_____

2. What's that? (beautiful, tiger)

_____

3. What's this? (big, room)

_____

4. What's that? (cold, drink)

_____

5. What's this? (small, cat)

_____

Listen and Write

lesson _lesson_ difficult _difficult_ easy _easy_

beautiful _beautiful_ interesting _interesting_ final _final_

big _big_ small _small_ cold _cold_

hot _hot_ It's hot. _It's hot._ It's cold. _It's cold._

It's a cold day today. _It's a cold day today._

That's an interesting zoo. _That's an interesting zoo._

English is difficult. _English is difficult._

This lesson is easy. _This lesson is easy._

Repeat

a giraffe	the giraffe	giraffes
a cat	the cat	cats
a dog	the dog	dogs
long	short	neck
big	small	head

The giraffe has a long neck.
The cat has a short neck.
The dog has a short neck.
The elephant has a big head.
The cat has a small head.

Practice

Answer the Questions

> **Example:** Is the classroom big? (No)
> <u>No, the classroom isn't big; it's small.</u>

1. Is the elephant small? (no)

   _____

2. Is the tiger small? (no)

   _____

3. Is that cat big? (no)

   _____

4. Is this dog small? (no)

   _____

5. Is that monkey big? (no)

   _____

Example: Is winter long? (yes)

<u>Yes, winter is long.</u>

1. Is summer hot? (yes)

_____

2. Is winter cold? (yes)

_____

3. Is the elephant's neck short? (yes)

_____

4. Is the dog's neck short? (yes)

_____

5. Is the giraffe's neck long? (yes)

_____

Command/Request

Example: Come in. (don't)

<u>Don't come in.</u>

1. Sit down. (don't)

_____

2. Open your books. (don't)

_____

3. Open the door. (don't)

_____

4. Close the door. (don't)

_____

5. Close the window. (don't)

_____

6. Open the window. (don't)

_____

Example: Come in please. (don't)
<u>Don't come in, please.</u>

1. Close the window, please. (don't)

_____

2. Open your books, please. (don't)

_____

3. Sit down, please. (don't)

_____

4. Open the door, please. (don't)

_____

5. Set the table, please. (don't)

_____

Example: Talk with me, please. (would)
<u>Would you talk with me, please?</u>

1. Play with us, please. (would)

_____

2. Come with me, please. (would)

_____

3. Study with them, please. (would)

_____

4. Practice with Hiromi and José, please. (would)

_____

5. Read your lesson, please. (would)

_____

Example: study (shall we now?)
<u>Shall we study now?</u>

1. read   _____

2. play   _____

3. sing   _____

4. talk   _____

5. travel   _____

6. work   _____

7. begin   _____

Example: study (let's, let's not, now)

Let's (not) study now.

1. worry   _____

2. go to the zoo   _____

3. play tennis   _____

4. read a book   _____

5. feed the animals   _____

Repeat:—these/those

Examples:

This is my sister Hiromi.

These are my sisters, Hiromi and Jane

That's a lion.

Those are lions.

This is an interesting book.
_____

That's a small dog.
_____

This is a big cat.
_____

That's a beautiful tiger.
_____

This is a strong horse.

_____

That's a small snake.

_____

This is a long neck.

_____

Exercises

Using and

Examples:

This is Hiromi.

That is José.

This is Hiromi, and that is José.

This is Ann.

That is Mike.

_____

This is Angel.

That is Manuel.

_____

 This is a cat.

That is a dog.

_____

 This is a book.

That is a pen.

_____

 These are pencils.

Those are notebooks.

_____

_____

 These are girls.

Those are boys.

_____

_____

 These are women.

Those are men.

_____

_____

Completion

Complete the dialogue. Use the words below.

four	months	summer	vacation	seasons

How many _____ are there in a year?

There are _____ seasons.

Each season has three _____ .

Students like the _____ season.

I know, it's _____ time.

these	those

This is my English book.

_____ here are Mike's.

That's my pencil.

_____ pencils are for my English class.

open	here	sit	come	that's	repeat

Mr. Powell: _____ in, please, Hiromi. _____ down.

Hiromi: _____'s my English book.

Mr. Powell: Please _____ it on page twenty-five.

Hiromi: _____ a difficult lesson, Mr. Powell.

Mr. Powell: O.K. _____ after me.

Make sentences with *and*

> **Example:** The book is on the table. The pencil is on the table.
> <u>The book and the pencil are on the table.</u>

1. The tiger is in the zoo. The lion is in the zoo.

_____

2. Mrs. Powell is an auto mechanic. George Sanches is an auto mechanic.

_____

3. José is doing his homework. Ann is doing her homework.

_____

4. The dog is in the house. The cat is in the house.

_____

5. Jane is Hiromi's sister. Yukio is Hiromi's brother.

_____

Unscramble

Unscramble the letters to make words.

> **Example:** macel = <u>camel</u>

yapl _____ nolg _____

asey _____ rwog _____

dnik _____ edef _____

eadh _____ dloc _____

litl _____ wlof _____

Answers to Unscramble:

play; long; easy; grow; kind; feed; head; cold; till; wolf

Puzzle

What is it? It's the beginning of the WINTER season. All of the words are animals (see following page).

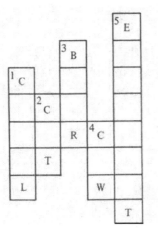

Down

1. It has a long neck and lives in the desert.
2. It is a house pet.
3. It is a big animal.
4. It gives us milk.
5. It's a very big animal.

Completion

Complete the reading using the words below.

| interesting | beautiful | in | summer | animals |

We are _____ a big zoo. The zoo is _____ . There are many _____ in the zoo. It is _____ to visit a zoo. It is _____ and there is no school.

Complete the talk using the words below.

| close | there's | open | read | look |

Mr. Powell: _____ your books to page thirty-nine.

Hiromi: _____ , it's a picture of a zoo.

Mr. Powell: Please, _____ the names of the animals.

Hiromi: _____ a lion and a camel.

José: . . . and there's a tiger and a monkey.

Mr. Powell: O.K. _____ your books. Now tell what you know about the animals.

Writing

Write a situation about the following dialogue.

Hiromi: Let's go to the zoo on Sunday.

José: I'm glad we're going.

Ann: Why are you glad?

José: We're studying about the animals, aren't we?

Write a dialogue about the following situation.

The phone rings.
You pick up the phone and say hello.
Your friend is on the phone.
He/she asks what you're doing.
You say you're reading the newspaper.
Your friend asks you to go to the movies.
You say that's a good idea.

Proverb

Monkey see, monkey do. (People like to do the things others do.)

CHAPTER SIX

It Surely Is Cold Today

IN THIS CHAPTER

Use of *and/but/or*

The weather: *cold/warm/mild/it rains/
it snows/it's windy/it's hot*

Directions: *North/South/East/West*

Continuation of Adjectives / Descriptive words

Compound Sentences

The Human Body

Read

Situation

It is the month of January in New York City. It is winter, and the weather is cold. Hiromi and Ann are visiting in New York. They wear heavy jackets and pants, but they are cold. The North wind makes their hands and feet freeze. The girls are at the airport. They are expecting the arrival of their friends José and Manuel.

Listen/Talk

Dialogue

José:	Brrr! I'm freezing!
Manuel:	Me, too. My feet are like ice.
José:	I think the snow is beautiful.
Manuel:	But why is it so cold?
Ann:	Stop complaining. Let's make a snowperson!
Hiromi:	Yes, let's have fun in the snow!

Copy

Winter _____ weather _____ cold _____

Winter weather is cold. _____

girls _____ at the _____ airport _____

The girls are at the airport. _____

expecting _____ arrival _____

They are expecting José. _____

freezing _____ I'm freezing. _____

feet _____ like _____ ice _____

My feet are like ice. _____

Listen and Write

It is January. The weather is cold. Hiromi and Ann are in New York City. Their hands and feet are freezing. The girls are at the airport. José and Manuel are arriving in New York.

Repeat—Who Is Who?

This is Hiromi.
Hiromi is thin.

This is Ann.
Ann is also thin.

Hiromi and Ann are thin.

This is Helen.
Helen is overweight.

This is Mike.
Mike is heavy.

Helen and Mike are fat.

This is Angel.
Angel is tall.

This is Alice.
Alice is also tall.

Angel and Alice are tall.

This is Lisa.
Lisa is short.

This is Ron.
Ron is also short.

Lisa and Ron are short.

This is Mr. Naga.
He's old.

This is Mrs. Naga.
She's also old.

Mr. and Mrs. Naga are old.

This is Mrs. Powell.
Mrs. Powell is young.

This is Mr. Powell.
Mr. Powell is also young.

Mr. and Mrs. Powell
are young.

This is a zoo.
The zoo is big.

This is an elephant.
An elephant is big.

The zoo and the
elephant are big.

This is a book.
The book is short.

This is a pencil.
The pencil is short.

The book and the pencil
are short.

This is Hiromi.
Hiromi is thin.

This is Mike.
Mike is overweight.

Hiromi is thin, but
Mike is fat.

This is Helen.
Helen is heavy.

This is Ann.
Ann is thin.

Helen is overweight,
but Ann is thin.

This is Angel.
Angel is tall.

This is Lisa.
Lisa is short.

Angel is tall, but Lisa
is short.

This is Alice.
Alice is tall.

This is Ron.
Ron is short.

Alice is tall, but Ron
is short.

This is Mr. Naga.
Mr. Naga is old.

This is Mrs. Powell.
Mrs. Powell is young.

Mr. Naga is old, but
Mrs. Powell is young.

This is Mrs. Naga.
Mrs. Naga is old.

This is Mr. Powell.
Mr. Powell is young.

Mrs. Naga is old, but
Mr. Powell is young.

Is this Hiromi or Ann?
This is Hiromi.

Is that Mike or Angel?
That is Mike.

 Is this Helen or Victoria?
This is Victoria.

Is that Ann or Alice?
That is Alice.

 Is this Donald or Yukio?
This is Donald.

Is that Donald or Yukio?
That is Yukio.

 Is this Mr. Naga or
Mr. Powell?
This is Mr. Naga.

Is that Mr. Powell
or Mr. Naga?
That is Mr. Powell.

Copy

thin _____ fat _____ tall _____ short _____

old _____ young _____ interesting _____

Hiromi is thin. _____

Hiromi and Ann are thin. _____

Mike is heavy. _____

Helen and Mike are overweight. _____

The zoo is interesting. _____

Listen and Write

Hiromi is thin. Her friend Ann is also thin. Helen and Mike are fat. Their English class is interesting. They like to study. They also like to play. On Saturday night they go to the movies.

Pronunciation Practice

Words

an airport	the airport	airports
an arrival	the arrival	arrivals
a jacket	the jacket	jackets
a wind	the wind	winds
a foot	the foot	feet

Questions

Is it January?

Is it Winter?

Is the weather cold?

Are Hiromi and Ann
   in New York?

Are they wearing jackets?

Are the girls cold?

Are they expecting José?

Statements

It is the month of January.

It is Winter.

The weather is cold.

Hiromi and Ann are
   in New York.

Hiromi and Ann are wearing jackets.

They are cold.

They are expecting José.

Questions

What month is it?

What season is it now?

Who is visiting in New York?

How is the weather?

What makes their hands
   and feet freeze?

Where are the girls?

Who is arriving?

Answers

It's the month of January.

It is the Winter season.

Hiromi and Ann are visiting.

The weather is cold.

The North wind makes their
   hands and feet freeze.

The girls are at the airport.

José and Manuel are arriving
   at the airport.

Practice—Describe

How Do I Look?

Examples: I'm Hiromi. <u>I'm thin.</u>
I'm Ann. <u>I'm also thin.</u>

I'm Helen.   _____

I'm Mike.   _____

I'm Angel.   _____

I'm Alice.   _____

I'm Lisa.   _____

I'm Ron.   _____

I'm Mr. Naga. _____

I'm Mrs. Naga. _____

I'm Mrs. Powell. _____

I'm Mr. Powell. _____

I'm _____ . _____

How Does It Look?

Example: This is a book. (interesting)
This book is interesting. It's an interesting book.

1. This is a zoo. (beautiful)

_____   _____

2. This is a school. (interesting)

_____   _____

3. This is a class. (big)

_____   _____

4. This is an office. (small)

_____   _____

5. This is a pencil. (short)

_____   _____

6. This is a pen. (long)

_____   _____

7. This is a bench. (short)

_____   _____

8. This is a bus. (wide)

_____   _____

9. This is a car. (narrow)

_____   _____

10. This is a hand. (large)

_____   _____

11. This is a lesson. (easy)

_____   _____

12. This is a word. (difficult)

_____   _____

Study

Use of **and/but/or**

Hiromi is thin. Yukio is thin.
Hiromi and Yukio are thin.

January is cold. February is cold.
January and February are cold.

June is warm. July is warm.
June and July are warm.

The North wind makes their hands freeze. It also makes their feet freeze.
The North wind makes their hands and feet freeze.

The elephant is big. The dog is small.
The elephant is big, but the dog is small.

The pencil is long. The pen is short.
The pencil is long, but the pen is short.

The bus is wide. The car is narrow.
The bus is wide, but the car is narrow.

The elephant is heavy. The cat is light.
The elephant is heavy, but the cat is light.

French is hard. English is easy.
French is hard, but English is easy.

It's raining today. It's snowing today.
Is it raining or is it snowing today?

It's cold in January. It's warm in January.
Is it cold or is it warm in January?

The pencil is long. The pencil is short.
Is the pencil long or is it short?

It snows in the winter. It rains in the winter.
Does it snow or does it rain in the winter?

This class is interesting. This class is not interesting.
Is this class interesting or is it not (isn't it) interesting?

Is it cold or is it hot in January?—It's cold.
Is Mr. Naga young or is he old?—Mr. Naga is old.
Is Hiromi fat or is she thin?—Hiromi is thin.
Is the elephant intelligent or dumb?—The elephant is intelligent.
Do we study chapter six or five?—We study chapter six.
Does Hiromi study English or French?—Hiromi studies English.
Does Mr. Naga speak English or Japanese?—Mr. Naga speaks English
    and Japanese.
Do we study English or Spanish?—We study English and Spanish.

Weather
It is cold in the Winter, and it snows.
It is warm in the Spring, and it rains.
It is hot in the Summer, and it rains.
It is mild in the Fall, and it is windy.

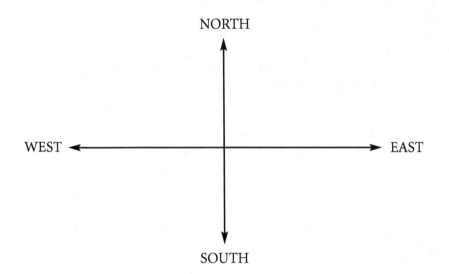

The WIND comes from the NORTH or from the SOUTH.

When the WIND comes from the NORTH, we call it the NORTH WIND.

When the WIND comes from the SOUTH, we call it the SOUTH WIND.

The WIND also comes from the WEST or the EAST.

What do we call the wind from the WEST? EAST?

_____

_____

_____

_____

Physical Descriptions

This is a person. His name is Mike Anderson.

Mike has:

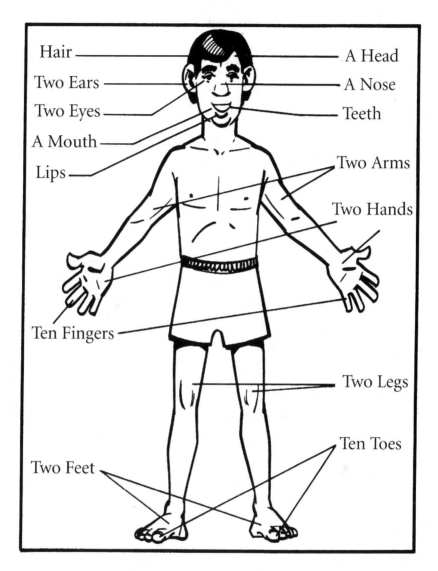

Hair — A Head
Two Ears — A Nose
Two Eyes — Teeth
A Mouth — Two Arms
Lips — Two Hands
Ten Fingers — Two Legs
Two Feet — Ten Toes

Practice

Answer the Questions

Example: How many fingers does Mike have? (ten)
Mike has <u>ten</u> fingers.

1. How many eyes does he have? (two)

_____

2. How many arms does he have? (two)

_____

3. How many legs does he have? (two)

_____

4. How many fingers does he have? (ten)

_____

5. How many toes does he have? (ten)

_____

Change to Many

Example: Mike's eye is small. = <u>Mike's eyes are small.</u>

1. Mike's foot is large. _____

2. Hiromi's finger is long. _____

3. Ann's toe is short. _____

4. Manuel's lip is thin. _____

5. Angel's tooth is white. _____

Example: The zoo is beautiful. = <u>The zoos are beautiful.</u>

1. The class is easy. _____

2. The teacher is interesting. _____

3. The student is intelligent. _____

4. The girl is beautiful. _____

5. The lesson is difficult. _____

6. The school is big. _____

7. The bus is wide. _____

8. The car is small. _____

9. The office is narrow. _____

10. The elephant is large. _____

Change to One

Example: The books are long. = <u>The book is long.</u>

1. The elephants are big. _____

2. The buses are wide. _____

3. The cars are narrow. _____

4. The jackets are warm. _____

5. The toes are short. _____

Example: Manuel's hands are big. = <u>Manuel's hand is big.</u>

1. Ann's arms are long. _____

2. Hiromi's classes are short. _____

3. Lisa's teeth are white. _____

4. José's lessons are easy. _____

5. These cars are beautiful. _____

6. Those students are intelligent. _____

7. These problems are hard. _____

8. Those animals are big. _____

Substitution Drill

1. Is this your **book** or is it that one?

> **class**
>
> **car**
>
> **dog**

2. Is that **Hiromi** or is it **Ann**?

> **José**   **Mike**?
>
> **Manuel**   **Ron**?
>
> **Helen**   **Alice**?

3. Is it **my** jacket or is it **yours**?
    Lisa's   **Ann's?**
    José's   **Manuel's?**
    Mike's   **Yukio's?**

4. Is the **elephant** big or small?
      lion
      tiger
      bus

5. Is **English** difficult or easy?
    Spanish
    French
    Polish

1. This is my **jacket,** and that one is hers.
        coat,
        book,
        class

2. This my **book,** and that one is Hiromi's.
        car,
        pencil,
        pen,

3. **Mr. Powell** is a **lawyer,** and **Hiromi** is a **student.**
Mrs. Powell	**doctor,**	**José**	
Mr. Naga	**salesman,**	**Yukio**	**salesman.**
Manuel	**secretary,**	**Mike**	**nurse.**

4. This class is **interesting,** and that one is too.
        small,
        large,
        a problem,

5. Lisa is **reading**, and Ann is **reading** too.
            playing,   **playing**
            walking,   **walking**
            studying,   **studying**

1. It is **January**, but it is not cold.
        February,
        March,
        December,

2. This class is **interesting**, but that one is not.
            large,
            small,
            a problem,

3. He's a good **teacher**, but he talks too loud.
            lawyer,
            mechanic,
            TV repairman,

4. It is a nice day today, but **Mike's** sick.
                Hiromi's
                Ann's
                Manuel's

5. This is a beautiful **car**, but it isn't mine.
              jacket,
              book,
              cat,

1.

| Give | the pencil
the pen
the book
the notebook | to | Hiromi,
Mrs. Powell,
Mr. Carson,
your friend, | please. |

2.

| Take | this jacket
this hat
these pants
this shirt
these shoes | to | her,
him,
them,
Mr. Powell,
Mrs. Carson, | please. |

3.

| Show | the class
the school
the cafeteria
the restaurant
the zoo | to | your friends,
my sister,
her brother,
his teacher,
their relatives, | please. |

4.

| Send | the letter
the book
the notebook
the tape recorder
your money | to | your mother,
her sister,
your teacher,
José,
me, | please. |

Exercises

Listen and Write

1. This is an English class. _____

2. That's my dog. _____

3. Give her your book, please. _____

4. Take this notebook to him. _____

5. Show me your letter. _____

Fill in the Blanks

Fill in *and/but/or*

Example: The zoo is big. The city is big.
<u>The zoo and the city are big.</u>

1. The cat is small. The dog is small.

_____

2. The car is good. The tape recorder is good.

_____

3. The book is interesting. The class is interesting.

_____

4. January is cold. February is cold.

_____

5. June is warm. July is warm.

_____

Compound Sentences

> **Example:** The car is small. The zoo is big.
> The car is small, but the zoo is big.

1. The elephant is big. The cat is small.

_____

2. The pencil is long. The pen is short.

_____

3. My class is interesting. Mike's class is not (isn't) interesting.

_____

4. My hat is beautiful. His hat is ugly.

_____

5. Hiromi's assignment is easy. José's assignment is hard.

_____

Change Statements to Questions

> **Example:** It's an easy lesson. It's a hard lesson.
> Is it an easy lesson or a hard lesson?

1. This book is interesting. This book is not (isn't) interesting.

_____

2. It's cold today. It's warm today.

_____

3. This is Hiromi's pen. This is Mike's pen.

_____

4. It's my jacket. It's Manuel's jacket.

_____

5. I'm going to class. I'm going to the zoo.

_____

6. It's raining today. It's snowing today.

_____

Unscramble

Unscramble the letters to make words.

Example: mra = <u>arm</u>

snoe _____	iarn _____
nsde _____	hows _____
pate _____	ylug _____
diew _____	dinw _____
dhae _____	dnha _____

Answers to Unscramble:

nose; rain; send; show; tape; ugly; wide; wind; head; hand

Change to Negative

Example: It's cold today.—<u>It isn't cold today.</u>

1. That's a hard textbook. _____

2. It's a big lion. _____

3. This is a small car. _____

4. That's a good tape recorder. _____

5. It's raining today. _____

6. It's snowing in May. _____

7. Hiromi's sick this morning. _____

8. José is studying hard. _____

9. Mike is a secretary. _____

10. Manuel is a TV repairman. _____

Change to **Positive**

Example: That's not an elephant.—<u>That's an elephant.</u>

1. This is not an easy class. _____

2. That's not a big car. _____

3. This is not an interesting zoo. _____

4. That's not a beautiful story. _____

5. Today's not a cold day. _____

6. Monday's not a work day. _____

7. Saturday's not a movie night. _____

8. Ann's not a good student. _____

9. Mrs. Carson's not a good doctor. _____

10. I'm not studying English. _____

Change to **Negative Questions**

Example: Are you a student?—<u>Aren't you a student?</u>

1. Are they in class? _____

2. Is she intelligent? _____

3. Is the zoo big? _____

4. Is the book interesting? _____

5. Does the giraffe have _____
   a long neck?

Change to Tag Questions

Example: It's big.—<u>It's big, isn't it?</u>

1. It's difficult. _____

2. He's intelligent. _____

3. They're cold. _____

4. Your feet are freezing. _____

5. Her eyes are big. _____

Example: It isn't hard.—<u>It isn't hard, is it?</u>

1. It isn't cold. _____

2. They're not at home. _____

3. It isn't difficult. _____

4. They're not in class. _____

5. You aren't studying. _____

Substitution Drill

1. This is an **English** class.
   French
   Spanish
   Chinese

2. The teacher is **Mr. Powell.**
     Mr. Reston.
     Ms. Zang.
     Mrs. Roland.

3. The class is important to **me.**
        him.
        her.
        us.

4. Is Mr. Powell a **good** teacher?
      interesting
      hard
      easy

5. **He's** an excellent teacher.
 Mr. Powell's
 Mrs. Roland's
 Mr. Reston's

Extra Dialogue

José: Good morning. Is this the English class?
Hiromi: Yes, it is.
José: Who's our teacher?
Hiromi: It's Mr. Powell.
José: Is he an interesting teacher?
Hiromi: Yes, he's great!
José: You really like him, don't you?
Hiromi: I certainly do. Everybody does.

Extra Story

Letter from Moshi

Dear Friends,
My name is Moshi Salinas. I'm from Mexico City, but right now I'm living in Monterrey. I'm studying English because it is important. When I learn English I hope to become a pilot and return to Mexico.

Answer Questions

1. Who's writing the letter?
2. Where's Moshi from?
3. What is Moshi studying?
4. Where's Moshi living now?
5. Why is Moshi studying English?

Exercises

Puzzle

This puzzle tells about the weather. To discover what kind of weather it is, complete all words *across*.

1. It's not cold and it isn't hot.
2. It's the cold season.
3. It's where the sun goes down.
4. The time when you use the umbrella.
5. The time when you put on extra clothing.
6. It's where the sun rises.
7. It's where most of the time it is warm.

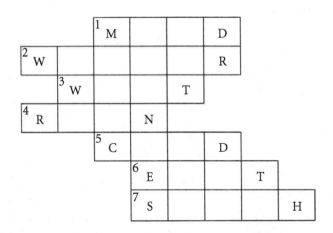

Completion

Complete the reading using the words below.

airport   heavy   hands   feet   visiting
weather   month

It is the _____ of January. The _____ is cold.
Hiromi and Ann are _____ in New York. They wear
_____ jackets. Their _____ and _____
freeze. The girls are at the _____ .

Complete the talk using the words below.

make   in   cold   me   my   freezing   beautiful

José: Brrr! I'm _____ !
Manuel: _____ too. _____ feet are like ice.
José: The snow is _____ .
Manuel: But why is it so _____ ?
José: Let's _____ a snowperson!
Manuel: Yes, let's have fun _____ the snow!

Listen and Write

the month _____ of January _____
It is the month of January. _____
winter _____ weather _____ cold _____
Winter weather is cold. _____
they're _____ visiting _____ New York _____
They're visiting in New York. _____
girls _____ at the _____ airport _____
The girls are at the airport. _____

Identify

Describe Using and

Example:

This is Hiromi.
Hiromi is thin.

    This is Ann.
    Ann is also thin.

<u>Hiromi and Ann are thin.</u>

This is Helen.
Helen is fat.

    This is Mike.
    Mike is also fat.

_____

This is Angel.
Angel is tall.

    This is Alice.
    Alice is also tall.

_____

This is Ron.
Ron is short.

    This is Lisa.
    Lisa is also short.

_____

This is Mrs. Powell.
Mrs. Powell is young.

This is Mr. Powell.
Mr. Powell is also young.

_____

This is Mr. Naga.
Mr. Naga is old.

This is Mrs. Naga.
Mrs. Naga is also old.

_____

Use *but*

Example:

This is Hiromi.
Hiromi is thin.

This is Mike.
Mike is fat.

<u>Hiromi is thin, but</u>
<u>Mike is fat.</u>

This is Helen.
Helen is fat.

This is Ann.
Ann is thin.

_____

This is an elephant.
The elephant is big.

This is a cat.
The cat is small.

_____

_____

This is a book.
The book is short.

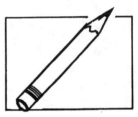

This is a pencil
The pencil is long.

_____

_____

This is Alice.
Alice is tall.

This is Ron.
Ron is short.

_____

_____

This is Mrs. Naga.
Mrs. Naga is old.

This is Mrs. Powell.
Mrs. Powell is young.

_____

How many?

This is a hand.
How many fingers does a hand have?

_____

This is a foot.
How many toes are there?

_____

This is a face.
How many eyes are there?

_____

This is a head.
How many ears are there?

_____

This is a person.
How many arms? Legs?

_____

_____

Writing

Write a dialogue about the following situation.

You greet your friend.
Your friend greets you.
You tell your friend about the beautiful zoo.
Your friend says "Let's go on Sunday."
You say it's O.K.
Your friend says goodbye.
You say "see you on Sunday."

Write a situation about the following dialogue.

How's the English class?
Very interesting.
Do you have a good teacher?
Certainly. It's Mr. Reston.
Mr. Reston? Is he new?
Yes, he begins tomorrow.

Proverb

Haste makes waste. (Always take your time!)

CHAPTER SEVEN

At the Supermarket

IN THIS CHAPTER

Use of *and/too*

Colors: *brown/red/white/black/yellow/blue/ orange/green/grey*

Use of *everybody/nobody*

Use of *as . . . as*

Use of *around/in/on/to/with*

Read

Situation

Mrs. Powell and her daughter Helen go grocery shopping on Monday. They do this together every Monday evening. The supermarket is around the corner. Mrs. Powell makes a shopping list. She buys some meat for dinner. Helen buys bread and butter. Mrs. Powell is looking for milk and some vegetables. They buy apples and pears for Mr. Powell. Everybody at home likes fruit.

Listen/Talk

Dialogue

Mrs. Powell:	A pound of hamburger meat, please.
Butcher:	Here it is, one pound.
Mrs. Powell:	Thank you.
Butcher:	You're welcome.

*　　*　　*

Helen: A loaf of bread, please.

Baker: Sliced?

Helen: Yes, please.

Baker: Here you are.

Helen: Thanks.

        *   *   *

Cashier: Is that all?

Mrs. Powell: Yes, it is.

Helen: How much is it?

Cashier: That's $8.26.

Mrs. Powell: Here's $10.00.

Cashier: Here's your change, $1.74.

Helen: Thanks. 'Bye now.

Cashier: Thank you. Come back soon.

Copy

Mrs. Powell's Grocery List

bread _____ sliced _____ loaf _____

One loaf of sliced bread. _____

milk _____ butter _____ cheese _____

hamburger _____ potato _____ soap _____

green beans _____ carrots _____ lettuce _____

tomato _____ kleenex _____ fruit _____

apples _____ pears _____ oranges _____

bananas _____ hot dogs _____

toilet paper _____ vegetables _____

Repeat

What's What?

What's this?
This is a loaf of bread.

What's that?
That's milk.

Bread is brown,
and milk is white.

What's this?
It's an apple.

What's that?
That's a pear.

Apples are red, and pears
are green.

What's this?
This is a carrot.

What's that?
That's a banana.

Carrots are orange, and
bananas are yellow.

 What's this?
It's a hamburger.

What's that?
That's a hot dog.

The hamburger is meat,
and the hot dog is meat.

 What's this?
This is lettuce.

What's that?
That's a tomato.

Lettuce is green,
and a tomato is red.

 What's this?
It's butter.

What's that?
That's cottage cheese.

Butter is yellow,
and cottage cheese is white.

 What's this?
This is soap.

What's that?
That's soup.

 What are these?
They're green beans.

What are those?
Those are carrots.

What's this?
It's an onion.

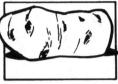
What's that?
That's a potato.

What's this?
It's an egg.

What's that?
That's a chicken.

What's He Selling?

What's he selling?
He's selling bicycles.

What's she selling?
She's selling bread.

What's he selling?
He's selling TVs.

What's he selling?
He's selling cars.

What's she selling?
She's selling books.

What's she selling?
She's selling meat.

What's he selling?
He's selling fruit.

What's he selling?
He's selling vegetables.

What's she selling?
She's selling milk.

What's she selling?
She's selling
orange juice.

Extra Dialogue

José: Pardon me. Where's the meat?
Cashier: The meat's in the first aisle.
José: Is it on the second shelf?
Cashier: No, it's with the chickens on the third shelf.
José: Thank you. I'm glad there's somebody to help me.

Answer the Questions

1. Who's buying meat?
2. In what aisle is the meat?
3. On which shelf is the meat?
4. Where are the chickens?
5. Is there somebody to help José?

Copy

pardon _____ me _____ Pardon me. _____

where's _____ meat _____ second _____ shelf _____

Where's the meat? _____

It's on the second shelf. _____

somebody _____ help _____ glad _____

I'm glad there's somebody to help me. _____

Pronunciation Practice

Words

an apple	the apple	apples
an onion	the onion	onions
a potato	the potato	potatoes
a bag	the bag	bags
a bread	the bread	breads
a pear	the pear	pears
kleenex	lettuce	milk
toilet	paper	yellow
red	brown	green

Questions

Where are we?

What are we doing?

What day is this?

Where's the supermarket?

Who makes a shopping list?

What does Mrs. Powell buy?

Who is looking for milk?

What do they buy for
Mr. Powell?

Statements

We're in a grocery store.

We're grocery shopping.

It's Monday.

The supermarket is around the corner.

Mrs. Powell makes a shopping list.

Mrs. Powell buys some meat.

Mrs. Powell is looking for milk.

They buy apples and pears.

Questions

Is Mrs. Powell grocery shopping?

Mrs. Powell's grocery shopping
on Monday, isn't she?

Answers yes/no

Yes, she is. Mrs. Powell is
grocery shopping.

Yes, she is.

Mrs. Powell's grocery shopping on Thursday, isn't she?	No, she isn't.
Mrs. Powell and Helen are grocery shopping together, aren't they?	Yes, they are.
Is the supermarket around the corner?	Yes, it is. Yes, the supermarket is around the corner.
Does Mrs. Powell make a shopping list?	Yes, she does. Yes, Mrs. Powell makes a shopping list.
Does Mrs. Powell buy some meat for dinner?	Yes, Mrs. Powell buys some meat for dinner.
Mrs. Powell buys some meat for dinner, doesn't she?	Yes, she does.
Helen buys bread and butter, doesn't she?	Yes, she does. Yes, Helen buys bread and butter.
Is Mrs. Powell looking for milk and some vegetables?	Yes, she is. Yes, Mrs. Powell is looking for milk and some vegetables.
Do they buy apples and pears for José?	No, they don't. No, they don't buy apples and pears for José.
Does everybody like fruit?	Yes, everybody likes fruit.

Repeat

What Color?

What color is a loaf of bread?
What color is it?
It's *brown*.
Color it brown.

What color is an apple?
What color is it?
It's *red*.
Color it red.

What color is milk?
What color is it?
It's *white*.
Color it white.

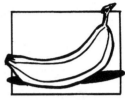

What color are bananas?
What color are they?
They're *yellow*.
Color them yellow.

What color is my coat?
What color is it?
It's *black*.
Color it black.

What color are his shoes?
What color are they?
They're *brown*.
Color them brown.

What color are the oranges?
What color are they?
They're *orange*.
Color them orange.

What color are her eyes?
What color are they?
They're *blue*.
Color them blue.

What color is your coat?
What color is it?
It's *grey*.
Color it grey.

What color is my hat?
What color is it?
It's *green*.
Color it green.

What color is his jacket?
What color is it?
It's *brown*.
Color it brown.

What color is your shirt?
What color is it?
It's *red*.
Color it red.

What color are my pants?
What color are they?
They're *yellow*.
Color them yellow.

Practice

Use of and/too

Examples: Mrs. Powell's going grocery shopping.
Helen's going grocery shopping.
Mrs. Powell's going grocery shopping, and Helen is too.

José is a student. Hiromi is a student.
José is a student, and Hiromi is too.

1. The supermarket is around the corner. The school is around the corner.

_____

2. Manuel's eating breakfast. Ann's eating breakfast.

_____

3. Alice likes fruit. Ron likes fruit.

_____

4. The supermarket is big. The zoo is big.

_____

5. Helen buys bread. Helen buys butter.

_____

Use of everybody/nobody

Mike tells about himself.

I am a student.

I study English. I understand Spanish and English.

I eat good food in the morning. I go shopping at the supermarket.

I read Spanish and English books.

Angel tells about Mike:

He is a student. He studies English. He understands Spanish and English.

He eats good food in the morning. He goes shopping at the supermarket.

He reads Spanish and English books.

Everybody/nobody is a student. *Everybody/nobody* studies English. *Everybody/nobody* understands Spanish and English. *Everybody/nobody* eats good food in the morning. *Everybody/nobody* goes shopping at the supermarket. *Everybody/nobody* reads Spanish and English books.

Examples: She reads a letter. (everybody)
<u>Everybody reads a letter.</u>

He plays tennis. (nobody)
<u>Nobody plays tennis.</u>

1. Mike likes Alice. (everybody)

_____

2. Hiromi likes reading. (nobody)

_____

3. Ron knows Manuel. (everybody)

_____

4. I like English. (everybody)

_____

5. We buy groceries at the supermarket. (everybody)

_____

Use of **around/in/on/to/with**

Where's the supermarket?
It's *around* the corner.

Where are the students?
They're *in* the classroom.

Is that my book *on* the table?
Yes, it is.

Aren't you going *to* the movies?
No, I have a lot of homework to do.

Who's going *with* you *to* the movies?
Hiromi and Manuel are going *with* me.

Write

1. . . . her hat   <u>What color is her hat?</u>   <u>What color is it?</u>

   . . . his jacket   _____   _____

   . . . their dog   _____   _____

   . . . his car   _____   _____

   . . . her hair   _____   _____

2. . . . my eyes   <u>What color are my eyes?</u>   <u>What color are they?</u>

   . . . his pants   _____   _____

   . . . her shoes   _____   _____

   . . . our pens   _____   _____

   . . . his pencils   _____   _____

3. . . . his hat . . . your jacket   <u>His hat is the same color as your jacket.</u>

   . . . her dress . . . his shirt   _____

   . . . their dog . . . our horse   _____

   . . . our bus . . . their car   _____

   . . . his pencil . . . my pen   _____

4. . . . my hat . . . his coat   <u>My hat is not the same color as his coat.</u>

    . . . his shirt . . . her dress   _____

    . . . her shoes . . . my jacket   _____

    . . . their pencils . . . our pens _____

    . . . our coats . . . your coats   _____

Extra Dialogue

Show me your hat.

This one?

No, the blue one.

It's the same color as my dress.

Everybody likes blue.

That's right. Everybody likes the same color.

Study

Use of as . . . as

What's this?

It's my car.

It's a beautiful car.

My car is as beautiful as his car.

What's that?

That's Ann's dog.

That's a big dog.

Ann's dog is as big as mine.

What's this?

It's Hiromi's dress.

It's a pretty dress.

Hiromi's dress is as pretty as Lisa's.

What's that?
That's a horse.
That's a strong horse.
That horse is as strong as mine.

What's this?
It's Manuel's jacket.
It's a large jacket.
Manuel's jacket is as large as yours.

Copy

dress _____ pretty _____ as _____ mine _____

Her dress is as pretty as mine. _____

jacket _____ expensive _____

His jacket is as expensive as mine. _____

dog _____ cat _____ big _____

The dog is as big as the cat. _____

Practice

Example: My hat is expensive. (yours)
<u>My hat is as expensive as yours.</u>

1. Hiromi's dress is pretty. (Ann's)

_____

2. Manuel's book is interesting. (José's)

_____

3. The Carson's home is big. (ours)

_____

4. Oranges are good. (bananas)

_____

5. Hamburgers are delicious. (hot dogs)

_____

Substitution Drill

1. Mike's car is as **pretty** as Manuel's.
       big
       expensive

2. Your lesson is as **easy** as mine. Let's study together.
       difficult
       interesting

3. My book is **on the desk**. Please bring it to **me**.
       in the office.   **the classroom.**
       under the chair.   **Hiromi's home.**

4. Mike's jacket is **brown**.
       green.
       black.

5. **Is** your **hat** the same color as mine?
       dress
  Are **shoes**
       eyes

6.

What color	is / are		Is / Are	it / they	
	is	**the dress?**	Is	it	**black?**
		the hat?			**red?**
		the jacket?			**brown?**
What color	are	**the oranges?**	Are	they	**yellow?**
		her eyes?			**blue?**
		his eyes?			**green?**

Practice

Colors

> ***Example:*** This is a banana. (yellow)
> <u>The banana is yellow.</u>
> <u>It is yellow.</u>

1. This is an apple. (red)

_____

_____

2. This is a loaf of bread. (brown)

_____

_____

3. That's a coat. (black)

_____

_____

4. This is my shirt. (brown)

_____

_____

5. That's her jacket. (blue)

_____

_____

6. Ann has a book. (blue)

_____

_____

7. That's Hiromi's hat. (green)

_____

_____

> ***Example:*** These are Mike's jackets. (brown)
> <u>These are Mike's brown jackets.</u>
> <u>They're brown.</u>

1. Ann has two eyes. (blue)

_____

_____

2. These are my shoes. (black)

_____

_____

3. Those are Mike's pants. (green)

_____

_____

4. There are apples on the shelf. (red)

_____

_____

5. These are bananas. (yellow)

_____

_____

What Are They Doing?

Example: This is Mr. Naga in his bicycle shop.
What is he doing? (selling bicycles)
<u>He is selling bicycles.</u>

This is Mrs. Brown in her butcher store.
What is she doing? (selling meat)

_____

That's Mrs. Smart in her bookstore.
What is she doing? (selling books)

_____

This is Mrs. Hassan in her bakery.
What is she doing? (selling bread)

_____

That's Mr. Vargas at his vegetable stand.
What is he doing? (selling vegetables)

_____

This is Mr. Anderson in his drugstore.
What is he doing? (selling medicine)

_____

This is Doctor Carson in her office.
What is she doing? (examining a patient)

_____

This is Isaac Betancourt.
What's he doing? (playing soccer)

_____

This is Mike Anderson.
What's he doing? (examining a patient)

_____

This is Mr. Powell.
What is he doing? (teaching a class)

_____

Extra Dialogue

Who's that short man over there?
You mean the man next to Mike?
No, not that one.
Then, is it the one with the red jacket?
Yes, that's the one.
Oh, that's Angel Lopez.
He's real cute.

Repeat
Who's That?—Who's This?

Who's that?
That's Mr. Powell,
our teacher.
Oh, yes, I know.
Mr. Powell's young.

Who's this?
Don't you know?
It's Hiromi. Hiromi is thin.

Who's that?
That's Ann Carson.
Ann Carson?
Yes, she's Hiromi's friend.

Who's this?
It's Helen.
Helen who?
Helen Powell.

Who's that?
You mean that fat man
over there?
Yes, that's the one.
It's Mike Anderson. He's fat.

Who's this?
It's nobody you know.
Well, who is it?
It's Angel Lopez, the TV repairman.

Who's that?
You mean that tall girl next to Mike?
Yes, that's the one I mean.
That's my friend Alice.

Who's this?
I don't know.
Let's ask Alice.
Oh, now I know. It's Ron.
He's the short one.

Who's that?
Everybody knows who that is.
I don't. I mean the thin man next to Ron.
Oh, that's José. He's a student.

How Much?

These are fresh onions.
How much are they?
    They're 3 lb. for $3.50.
    They're three pounds for three dollars and fifty cents.

These are fresh,
juicy lemons.
How much are they?
They're two for one dollar.

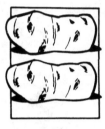

These are extra big potatoes.
How much are they?
They're 5 lb. for $4.00.
They're five pounds
for four dollars.

This is fresh cottage cheese.
How much is it?
It's $2.00 for a carton.
It's two dollars for a carton.

This is fresh farm celery.
How much is it?
It's $2.00.

This is good coffee.
How much is it?
I don't know.
It's expensive.

These are juicy, ripe tomatoes.
How much are they?
    They're three pounds for four dollars.
    They're 3 lb. for $4.00.

These are fresh, juicy oranges.
How much are they?
They're 3 lb. for $4.00.
They're three pounds for four dollars.

This is corn.
How much is it?
It's five ears for four dollars.

These are delicious apples.
How much are they?
They're 3 lb. for $4.00.
They're three pounds for four dollars.

This is good hamburger meat.
How much is it?
It's very expensive.

This is frozen orange juice.
How much is it?
It's $3.39 for ½ gal.
It's three dollars and thirty-
nine cents for half a gallon.

These are fresh fish.
How much are they?
They're expensive.

This is real butter.
How much is it?
It's not expensive.
It's also not cheap.

This is toilet soap.
How much is it?
It's not cheap.
It's not expensive.

This is soft toilet paper.
How much is it?
It's not cheap.
It's expensive.

These are ripe bananas.
How much are they?
They're 4 lb. for $1.00.
They're four pounds
for one dollar.

This is good beer.
How much is it?
It's cheap.
It's not expensive.

These are eggs.
How much are they?
They're expensive.

How Are They?

These are apples.
How are these apples?
They're delicious apples.

These are oranges.
How are these oranges?
They're juicy, fresh oranges.

This is soft toilet paper.
How is this toilet paper?
It's soft toilet paper.

These are ripe bananas.
How are these bananas?
They're ripe bananas.

This is good beer.
How is this beer?
It's good beer.

These are onions.
How are these onions?
They're fresh onions.

Those are lemons.
How are those lemons?
They're fresh and juicy lemons.

This is cottage cheese.
How is this cheese?
It's fresh cottage cheese.

This is celery.
How is this celery?
It's fresh farm celery.

This is coffee.
How is this coffee?
It's good coffee.

These are potatoes.
How are these potatoes?
They're extra big potatoes.

These are tomatoes.
How are those tomatoes?
They're juicy, ripe tomatoes.

This is orange juice.
How is this orange juice?
It's frozen orange juice.

This is hamburger meat.
How's this hamburger meat?
It's fresh hamburger meat.

These are fish.
How are these fish?
They're fresh fish.

Those are eggs.
How are those eggs?
They're fresh and extra large.

Study

Where Is?—Where Are?

You're in a supermarket. You're buying groceries. Where are the potatoes, onions, etc.? In a supermarket there are aisles. The aisles have numbers: aisle #1, #2, etc. There are also many shelves. The groceries are on the shelves. The shelves are in the aisles. The supermarket looks like this:

Now, answer the following questions.

Example:

These are apples.
Where are they?
<u>They're in aisle one on the lower shelf.</u>

These are oranges.
Where are they?

_____

This is toilet paper.
Where is it?

_____

Those are bananas.
Where are they?

_____

This is beer.
Where is it?

_____

Those are onions.
Where are they?

_____

These are lemons.
Where are they?

_____

This is cottage cheese.
Where is it?

_____

This is celery.
Where is it?

_____

This is coffee.
Where is it?

_____

These are potatoes.
Where are they?

_____

Those are tomatoes.
Where are they?

_____

This is orange juice.
Where is it?

_____

These are fish.
Where are they?

_____

This is hamburger meat.
Where is it?

_____

These are eggs.
Where are they?

_____

This is butter.
Where is it?

_____

This is milk.
Where is it?

_____

Exercises

Completion
Complete the reading using the words below.

around   together   on   for

Helen goes grocery shopping _____ Monday. Helen and her

mother go grocery shopping _____ . The supermarket is

_____ the corner. They buy groceries _____ dinner.

Complete the talk using the words below.

| you | please | of | thanks |

Helen: A loaf _____ bread, please.

Baker: Sliced?

Helen: Yes, _____ .

Baker: Here _____ are.

Helen: _____ .

Unscramble
Unscramble the letters to make words.

Example: agb = <u>bag</u>

fshi _____   ramf _____

eatm _____   olaf _____

fost _____   lio _____

geg _____   ereb _____

ronc _____   prie _____

Answers to Unscramble:

fish; farm; meat; loaf; soft; oil; egg; beer; corn; ripe

Puzzle
This is the name of the place where you go to buy food.
Complete all words *down* (see puzzle on the following page).

1. Mrs. Powell and her daughter go there _____ .
2. It is the color of lettuce.
3. Bread comes in this color.
4. It's an orange vegetable.
5. It's the color of milk.
6. It is the color of an apple.
7. Bananas and butter are this color.

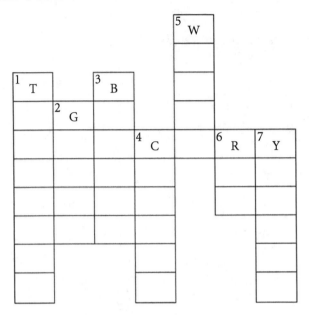

Listen and Write

coffee _____ good _____ fresh _____

This coffee is good. _____

It is fresh. _____

Where _____ are _____ eggs _____

Where are the eggs? _____

loaf _____ sliced _____ bread _____

A loaf of sliced bread. _____

Write a dialogue about the following situation.

You are in a supermarket.
You ask the baker for bread.
He asks you how you like it.
You tell him you like it sliced.
He gives you the bread.
You thank him
He says good-bye.
You say good-bye.

Write a situation about the following dialogue.

Who's that man over there?
The short one?
No, the tall one.
The tall one in the red shirt?
No, in the green pants.
Oh, that's my friend Mike.
Introduce me, please.
O.K. Let's go.

Proverb

You are what you eat. (Eat well and feel well.)

CHAPTER EIGHT

Our Family

IN THIS CHAPTER

Object Pronouns (review)

Direct and Indirect Object

Nouns and Pronouns

Comparatives of Adjectives
and Adverbs

Use of *more/bigger/better/than*

Use of *too* + *Adverb*

Read

Situation

This is my family. My family is important to me. We have a family reunion every year. It happens on my grandmother's birthday. She is seventy-eight years old today. Grandfather is no longer alive. My Uncle Rubin and Aunt Yaffa are here from Houston. I also have cousins Harry and Aaron. We give presents to Grandmother, and she is happy. We give them to her every year. The reunion is bigger every year. The presents are better than the previous year, and they are more expensive. We sing "Happy Birthday" to Grandmother.

BIRTHDAY SONG

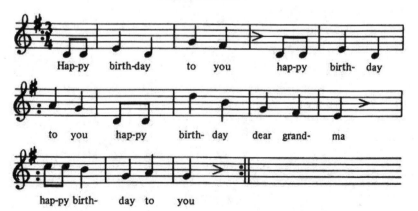

Hap-py birth-day to you hap-py birth-day

to you hap-py birth-day dear grand-ma

hap-py birth-day to you

Answer the Questions

1. What kind of song is this?
2. Whose birthday is it?
3. What do we tell grandmother?

Listen/Talk

Dialogue

Harry:	That's a nice song, isn't it?
Ann:	Yes, it's a happy song.
Harry:	Go ahead, give the present to Grandma.
Ann:	It's not mine. You give it to her.
Harry:	O.K., O.K., I hope she likes it.
Grandmother:	Thank you, children. I always like your presents.
Aaron:	I'm glad it's September, Grandma.
Grandmother:	So am I. I look forward to it.
Ann:	We hope you live to be a hundred.
Grandmother:	Oh, I don't think I'd like that.
Harry:	Why not, Grandma?
Grandmother:	My place is too small for the presents I get.

Copy

this _____ is _____ our _____ family _____
This is our family. _____
aunt _____ uncle _____ brother _____ sister _____
He's my brother. _____
She's his sister. _____
This is Uncle William. _____
That's my Aunt Jenny. _____
we _____ give _____ presents _____ grandmother _____
We give presents on birthdays. _____
they _____ sing _____ happy _____ birthday _____
They sing "Happy Birthday." _____
nice _____ happy _____ song _____
That's a nice song. _____

MY FAMILY ALBUM
(Relationships)

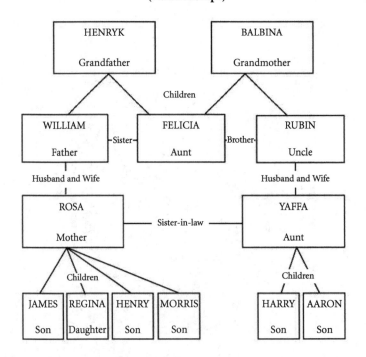

Repeat

Who Is Who?

Who's this?
This is Henryk.
Henryk is our grandfather.

Who's that?
That's Balbina.
Balbina is our grandmother.

Who's this?
This is William.
William is Henryk's son.
He's also Balbina's son.

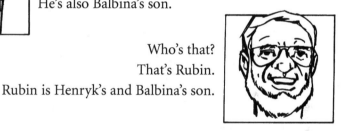

Who's that?
That's Rubin.
Rubin is Henryk's and Balbina's son.

Who's this?
This is Rosa.
Rosa is William's wife.

Who's that?
That's Yaffa.
Yaffa is Rubin's wife.

Who's this?
This is James.
James is the son of William and Rosa.
James is Rubin's nephew.

Who's that?
That's Regina.
Regina is James' sister.
She is the daughter of William and Rosa.
Regina is Rubin's and Yaffa's niece.

Who's this?
This is Henry.
Henry is Regina's brother.

Who's that?
That's Morris.
Morris is Henry's, Regina's and James' brother.

Who's this?
This is Harry.
Harry is Rubin's and Yaffa's son.
Harry is Regina's cousin.
Harry is William's nephew.

Who's that?
That's Aaron.
Aaron is Harry's brother.
He is Rubin's and Yaffa's son.
Aaron is William's and Rosa's nephew.
He is Henry's and Morris' cousin.

Meet My Family

 My name's William.

That's my wife, Rosa.

 This is my son, James.

That's my daughter, Regina.

 This is my son, Henry.

That's my son, Morris.

 This is my brother, Rubin.

That's Rubin's wife, Yaffa.
Yaffa is my sister-in-law.
I am Yaffa's brother-in-law.

 This is my nephew, Harry.

That's Harry's brother, Aaron.
Aaron's also my nephew.

 This is my father, Henryk.

That's my mother, Balbina.

This is my son, James.
James is Henryk's grandson.

This is my daughter, Regina.
Regina's Balbina's
granddaughter.

Extra Dialogue

Barry: Gloria, meet my cousin, Pat.
Gloria: Nice to meet you, Pat.
Pat: Same here. Do you have a sister?
Gloria: Yes, I do.
Pat: Is she older than you?
Gloria: Why do you ask?
Pat: Because you're too young for me.

Answer the Questions

1. Who's Barry?
2. Who's Pat?
3. Does Gloria have a sister?
4. Is Gloria's sister older or younger?
5. Is Pat older than Gloria?

Copy

grandfather _____ father _____ mother _____
husband _____ wife _____ nephew _____
niece _____ cousin _____ in-law _____
old _____ older _____ young _____ younger _____
Grandfather Henryk is old. _____
Grandmother Balbina is older than Henryk. _____
Cousin Harry is young. _____
Cousin Aaron is younger than Harry. _____

Pronunciation Practice

Words

family	a family	my family
wife	my wife	his wife
husband	my husband	her husband
child	a child	children
cousin	my cousin	his cousin
nephew	her nephew	his nephew
niece	my niece	his niece

Questions

Who am I?

Who's that?

Who's this?

Who's she?

Who's he?

Where's your brother?

What's this?

What do we have?

When is the reunion?

Where are they from?

What do we give on birthdays?

How are the presents?

How big is the reunion?

What do we sing?

Statements

You're my older brother.

That's his younger sister.

This is Henry's sister Regina.

She's my cousin Zenia.

He's her nephew Isaac.

My brother is at school.

That's my family.

We have a family reunion.

It happens every year.

They're from Houston.

We give presents.

They are more expensive every year.

It is bigger every year.

We sing "Happy Birthday."

Questions

Is this your family?

This is your family, isn't it?

Is Grandfather alive?

Grandfather's alive, isn't he?

Are your cousins here?

Is Rubin your uncle?

Answers

Yes, it is.

No, it isn't.

Yes, he is.

No, he isn't.

Yes, my cousins are here.

Yes, he is. Rubin is my uncle.

Questions	Answers
Questions	*Answers*
Rubin is your uncle, isn't he?	No, Rubin's not my uncle.
Aaron and Harry are your cousins, aren't they?	Yes, they are. Aaron and Harry are my cousins.
Do you give presents to Grandmother?	Yes, we do. We give her presents.
Is the reunion bigger every year?	Yes, it is. The reunion is bigger every year.
Are the presents more expensive?	Yes, they are more expensive.
Presents are more expensive, aren't they?	No, they aren't. Yes, they are.
Do you sing for your grandmother?	Yes, we sing for Grandmother.
You sing for your grandmother, don't you?	No, we don't. Yes, we do.

Study

Pronouns (Review)

Possessives

		subject	object		determiner	pronoun
1st person	singular	I	me		my	mine
	plural	we	us		our	ours
2nd person	singular	you			your	yours
	plural					
3rd person	singular masculine	he	him		his	
	singular feminine	she	her		her	hers
	singular non-personal	it			its	
	plural		they	them	their	theirs

Noun and Pronoun Objects

We have a *family reunion* every year. (Noun Object)
We have *it* every year. (Pronoun Object)

We give *presents* to *Grandmother*. (Noun Objects)
We give *them* to *her*. (Pronoun Objects)

Give *Harry* the *present*. (Noun Objects)
Give *it* to *him*. (Pronoun Objects)

I write a *letter* to my *friend*. (Noun Objects)
I write *it* to *him*. (Pronoun Objects)

We sing a *song* for *Grandmother*. (Noun Objects)
We sing *it* for *her*. (Pronoun Objects)

I hope *Harry* likes the *present*. (Noun Objects)
I hope *he* likes *it*. (Pronoun Objects)

My place is too small for the *presents*. (Noun Object)
My place is too small for *them*. (Pronoun Object)

Adjectives (Review)
Adjectives describe *what kind, how many,* and *which one.*

What Kind
There is a *big* cake on the table.
Harry gives Grandmother a *beautiful* present.
Aaron is a *good* student.
Hiromi is a *beautiful* girl.
José is a *quick* runner.

How Many
There are *seventeen* students in the classroom.
She buys *ten* notebooks.
I have *one* pen.
Ann has *no* classes on Saturday.
There are *three* restaurants on this street.

Which One
Is this your *first* day of school?
No, it is my *third* day.
He is *second* in line.
On the *fifth* of August we have a picnic.
The *fourth* of July is a holiday.

Adverbs

Adverbs answer the questions *how, when,* and *where.*

How

How are you?	I'm *fine,* thank you.
How does Hiromi talk?	Hiromi talks *fast.*
How does José study?	José studies *hard.*
How do they write?	They write *well.*
How does Mr. Powell explain?	Mr. Powell explains *carefully.*

When

When do you begin school?	We begin school *early.*
When does Ann come to class?	Ann comes to class *late.*
When do you get up?	I get up *on time.*
When does he study?	He studies *late.*

Where

Where is the English class?	It's over *there.*
Where are the students?	They're *here.*
Where is Hiromi?	She's over *here.*
Where is Isaac?	He's *here.*

Add *-ly* to make an *Adverb*

Adjective	*Adverb*
careful	careful*ly*
easy	easi*ly*

glad	glad*ly*
happy	happi*ly*
quick	quick*ly*
slow	slow*ly*
wise	wise*ly*

Comparison of *Adjective*—Use *Than*
Add *-er* or the word *more*.

It's a *nice* day today. (adjective)
It's a *nicer* day than yesterday. (comparative)

This lesson is *easy*. (adjective)
My lesson is *easier* than yours. (comparative)

The family reunion is *big*. (adjective)
The reunion gets *bigger* every year. (comparative)

This is a *happy* family. (adjective)
My family is *happier* than yours. (comparative)

Angel has a *fast* car. (adjective)
Alice has a *faster* car than Angel. (comparative)

The presents are *expensive*. (adjective)
The presents are *more (less) expensive* every year. (comparative)

This is a *beautiful* book. (adjective)
Your book is *more (less) beautiful* than mine. (comparative)

That's an *interesting* class. (adjective)
His class is *more (less) interesting* than hers. (comparative)

Oranges are *delicious*. (adjective)
Apples are *more (less) delicious* than oranges. (comparative)

Comparison of Adverb
Adverbs have the same rules of comparison as *adjectives*. Some adverbs have the same form as adjectives:

early   late   hard   slow   fast   etc.

This is an *early* class. (adjective)
He comes *early* to class. (adverb)
He comes *earlier* to class than I. (adverb comparison)

That's a *late* show on TV. (adjective)
Ann studies *late*. (adverb)
Ann studies *later* than Hiromi. (adverb comparison)

This is a *hard* lesson. (adjective)
You study *hard*. (adverb)
I study *harder* than he. (adverb comparison)

He is a *careful* driver. (adjective)
He drives *carefully*. (adverb)
Alice drives *more carefully* than Lisa. (adverb comparison)

José is a *slow* learner. (adjective)
José learns *slowly*. (adverb)
I learn *more slowly* than José. (adverb comparison)

That's a *fast* car. (adjective)
He's driving *fast*. (adverb)
Manuel drives *faster* than Isaac. (adverb comparison)

Use of too + adverb
Slow down, you're driving *too fast*.
Relax, you're studying *too hard*.
You have an exam tomorrow, don't come home *too late*.
My place is *too small*.
The family reunion is getting *too big*.

Extra Dialogue

Barry: Hello, Dan. How are you?
Dan: Uh, fine, thanks. How about you?
Barry: Very well, thanks. My wife's sick, though.

Dan: Oh! I'm sorry to hear that.

Barry: She's seeing a doctor every day.

Dan: Hope she gets to feel better.

Barry: Thanks, see you later.

Dan: See you, Barry.

Answer the Questions

1. Whose wife is sick?
2. Where is she going every day?
3. Who is Dan's friend?
4. What does Dan hope?

Repeat—Who are They?

This is Harry.
He is Aaron's brother.
He is the son of Rubin and Yaffa.

This is Aaron.
He is Harry's brother.
He is the nephew of William and Rosa.

This is Yaffa.
Yaffa is Rubin's wife.
She's the mother of Harry and Aaron.

This is Rosa.
She's Henry's mother.
She's William's wife.
Rosa is Harry's and Aaron's aunt.

That's William.
He's Rosa's husband.
He's the uncle of Harry and Aaron.

That's Rubin.
Rubin is William's brother.
He is the uncle of his brother's children.

This is Henryk.
He's William's father.
He's also Rubin's father.
Henryk is Harry's grandfather.

That's Balbina.
Balbina is Henryk's wife.
She's Morris' grandmother.

Practice

Who am *I?*

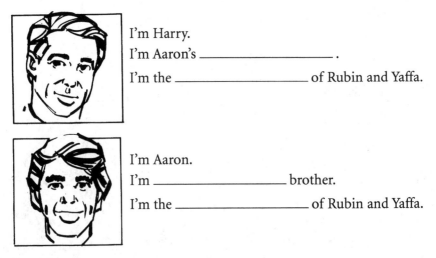

I'm Harry.
I'm Aaron's _____ .
I'm the _____ of Rubin and Yaffa.

I'm Aaron.
I'm _____ brother.
I'm the _____ of Rubin and Yaffa.

I'm Yaffa.

I'm _____ wife.

I'm the _____ of Harry and Aaron.

I'm Rosa.

I'm the _____ of Henry.

I'm William's _____ .

I'm Harry's and Aaron's _____ .

I'm William.

I'm the _____ of Henry and Morris.

I'm the _____ of Harry and Aaron.

I'm Rubin.

I'm Yaffa's _____ .

I'm the _____-_____ of Rosa.

I'm Ann Carson.

I'm the _____ of Mr. Carson.

Doctor Carson is my _____ .

I'm Hiromi.

I'm the _____ of Yukio.

I'm the _____ of Mr. and Mrs. Naga.

I'm Isaac.

I'm José's _____ .

I'm the _____ of Mr. and Mrs. Betancourt.

Victoria is my _____ .

Direct Object Nouns *and* Pronouns

Example: I see Mrs. Naga. (Noun Object)
I see <u>her</u>. (Pronoun Object)

1. Mike brings a present.   Mike brings presents.
   Mike brings _____ . Mike brings _____ .

2. Ann greets Mrs. Naga.   Ann greets Mr. and Mrs. Naga.
   Ann greets _____ . Ann greets _____ .

3. Isaac kicks a soccer ball.   Isaac kicks soccer balls.
   Isaac kicks _____ . Isaac kicks _____ .

4. Harry likes Morris.   Harry likes Morris and Henry.
   Harry likes _____ . Harry likes _____ .

5. Grandmother likes the family.   We are Grandmother's family.
   Grandmother likes _____ . She likes _____ .

6. We like our cousin Harry.   We like our cousins Harry and Aaron.
   We like _____ . We like _____ .

7. I see my sister-in-law.   I see my sister and brother-in-law.
   I see _____ . I see _____ .

8. We hear the noise.   They hear the noises.
   We hear _____ . They hear _____ .

9. Harry's buying the car.   Harry's looking at cars.

   Harry's buying _____ . Harry's looking at _____ .

10. We like our family reunion.   They like family reunions.

   We like _____ . They like _____ .

Substitution Drill

1. Give the present to **her**.
       me.
       him.
       us.

2. Tell **me** a story.
    him
    her
    us
    them

3. Write **her** a letter.
     him
     me
     us
     them

4. Excuse **me**, please.
     him,
     her,
     us,

5. Don't forget **me**.
     her.
     him.
     us.
     them.

6. Give it to **us**.
       me.
       him.
       her.

7. Show **me** the lesson.
      him
      her

8. Give me the **book**.
       present.
       football.
       money.

Exercises

Object Pronoun

Example: Do you see <u>Brian?</u>
Do you see <u>him?</u>

1. Remember <u>Grandmother.</u>
Remember _____ .

2. Bring <u>the book.</u>
Bring _____ .

3. Study <u>the lesson.</u>
Study _____ .

4. Remember <u>Harry.</u>
Remember _____ .

5. Pardon <u>your friends.</u>
Pardon _____ .

6. Close <u>the door.</u>
Close _____ .

7. Repeat <u>the words.</u>
Repeat _____ .

8. Write <u>a story.</u>
Write _____ .

9. Learn from <u>experience.</u>
Learn from _____ .

10. Do <u>your work.</u>
Do _____ .

Two Pronouns Objects

Example: Tell the <u>children a story.</u>
Tell <u>it</u> to <u>them.</u>

1. Give <u>Grandmother the present.</u>

   Give _____ to _____ .

2. Write <u>mother a letter.</u>

   Write _____ to _____ .

3. Tell <u>Henry a story.</u>

   Tell _____ to _____ .

4. Sell <u>the man your car.</u>

   Sell _____ to _____ .

5. Tell <u>the students the news.</u>

   Tell _____ to _____ .

6. Give <u>Hiromi the homework.</u>

   Give _____ to _____ .

7. Write <u>Mike a letter.</u>

   Write _____ to _____ .

8. Please give <u>the notebook to Ann.</u>

   Please give _____ to _____ .

9. Please read <u>the letter to Manuel.</u>

   Please read _____ to _____ .

Adjective or Adverb

Use the correct form of the *adjective* or *adverb*.

Example: This is a <u>hard</u> (hard) lesson.

1. Morris drives _____ . (careful)

2. Mike is a _____ driver. (careful)

3. Ann studies _____ . (quick)

4. Lisa walks _____ . (slow)

5. Hiromi is a _____ girl. (beautiful)

6. Isaac writes _____ . (beautiful)

Use *As . . . As* or *Than*

Examples: Hiromi is more beautiful <u>than</u> Ann.
Ann is <u>as</u> beautiful <u>as</u> Lisa.

1. José studies faster _____ Manuel.

2. It's a nicer day _____ yesterday.

3. Angel is _____ careful _____ his friend.

4. Victoria's grandmother is happier _____ Harry's.

5. We study _____ hard _____ you.

6. He comes earlier to class _____ I.

7. Ann studies later _____ José.

8. We study harder _____ you.

9. Who is a better student _____ I?

10. Is he _____ careful _____ his brother?

Unscramble

Unscramble the letters to make words.

Example: lenuc = <u>uncle</u>

fyliam _____   bashund _____

pehnew _____   restis _____

othrebr _____   neurion _____

oungy _____   ons _____

nousic _____   rehfat _____

Answers to Unscramble: reunion; son; father.

family; nephew; brother; young; cousin; husband; sister;

Puzzle—Who Is It?

All the words relate to the family.—Complete all words *down.*

1. You live together in the same house.
2. He is the son of your uncle.
3. She is the daughter of your parents.
4. He is married to your mother.
5. He is your brother's son.
6. He is also the son of your parents.

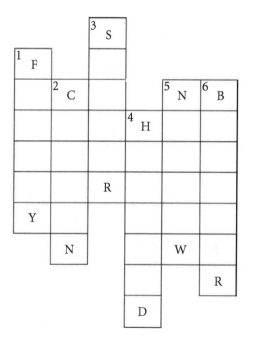

What's the Relationship?

Example:

You're William.
What's your relationship to her?
<u>I'm Jenny's husband.</u>
<u>She's my wife.</u>

You're Jenny.
What's your relationship to him?
I'm _____ .
He's _____ .

You're Aaron.
What's your relationship to him?
I'm _____ .
He's _____ .

You're Henry.
What's your relationship to him?
I'm _____ .
He's _____ .

You're Aaron.
What's your relationship to her?
I'm _____ .
She's _____ .

You're Yaffa.
What's your relationship to him?
I'm _____ .
He's _____ .

You're Rubin.
What's your relationship to him?
I'm _____ .
He's _____ .

You're Rubin.
What's your relationship to her?
I'm _____ .
She's _____ .

You're Aaron.
What's your relationship to him?
I'm _____ .
He's _____ .

You're Sharon.
What's your relationship to him?
I'm _____ .
He's _____ .

You're Aaron.
What's your relationship to her?
I'm _____ .
She's _____ .

You're Balbina.
What's your relationship to her?
I'm _____ .
She's _____ .

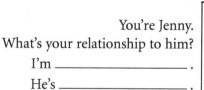

You're Jenny.
What's your relationship to him?
I'm _____ .
He's _____ .

You're Aaron.
What's your relationship to him?
I'm _____ .
He's _____ .

You're Yaffa.
What's your relationship to him?
I'm _____ .
He's _____ .

Completion

Complete the talk using the words below.

> happy   it   present   birthday   her

Manuel: It's Grandmother's _____ today.

Mike: Let's give her a _____ .

Henry: You give _____ to _____ , Mike.

Morris: What is _____ ?

Ann: It's a _____ song.

Talk about yourself.

Tell your name.
Tell who are your mother and father.
Tell who are your brothers and sisters.
Tell who are your cousins.
Tell who are your uncles and aunts.
Tell who are your grandfather and your grandmother.
Are you short?
Are you tall?
Are you thin?
Are you fat?

Listen and Write

bring _____ presents _____ party _____

We bring presents to the party. _____

have _____ family _____ reunion _____

We have a family reunion. _____

bigger _____ every _____ year _____

It's bigger every year. _____

cousins _____ here _____ visit _____

My cousins are here to visit. _____

Write a dialogue about the following situation.

It's your friend's birthday.
You're planning a birthday party with friends.
The party is on Saturday night.
There is food and music.
It's a surprise party.

Write a situation about the following dialogue.

Hey, this is a nice party.
I agree. This party is nicer than the last one.
Really? I don't remember.
You know, the one on September 19th.
Oh, yes. You're right. This is a nicer party.

Proverb

A family that plays together stays together.
(When you do things with your family you feel happy.)

Our Home

Review and Use of *Wh*—questions

Positions: *above/below/under/on top of/*
in front of/next to/beside/behind

Use of *a/an/the/some*

Comparison of Adjectives and Adverbs

Read

Situation

This is our home. It is beautiful. We live here, and we like it. There are three bedrooms in our house. One bedroom is on the first floor. The other two bedrooms are on the second floor. There are two bathrooms. One bathroom is downstairs, and the second one is upstairs. We have a family room, a kitchen, and a living room. The garage is next to the house. There is an extra room on top of the garage. There are trees in front of our house, and there are many pretty flowers.

Listen/Talk

Dialogue

José:	I really like your home.
Mr. Carson:	You're welcome to come anytime.
Ann:	Yes, come often.
José:	Whose car is it in front of the garage?
Ann:	Uh, it's mine. Want a ride?
José:	Yes, but there's a cat on top of it.
Ann:	That's only our pet, Mitzi.
José:	She's beautiful.
Ann:	She's a member of our family.

José: You really mean that?

Ann: What's the matter, don't you like cats?

José: Some are nice; others I don't care for.

Ann: Mitzi is wonderful.

José: I'm sure she is.

Copy

what _____ matter _____ mean _____

What's the matter? _____

What do you mean? _____

live _____ like _____ home _____ here _____

This is our home. _____

We like it here. _____

bathroom _____ bedroom _____ floor _____

There are two bathrooms. _____

We have three bedrooms. _____

downstairs _____ upstairs _____

The bathroom is downstairs. _____

Our bedroom is upstairs. _____

extra _____ room _____ on top _____

There's an extra room on top of the garage. _____

Repeat—What Is It?

What's this?
This is our home.
We live here.

What's that?
That's my bathroom.
I wash up in the bathroom.

What's this?
It's my bedroom.
I sleep there.

What's that?
That's our family room.
We watch TV here.

What's this?
This is our kitchen.
We cook our meals here.

What's that?
That's the living room.
Our guests visit here.

What's this?
It's the garage.
We keep our car here.

What's that?
That's our car.
We drive it on trips.

What are these?
These are our trees.
They give us shade.

What are those?
Those are our flowers.
They make our house look pretty.

What's this?
It's our cat.
She's our house pet.

What's that?
That's our dog.
He watches our home.

What's this?
It's a door.
There are doors in every room.

What's that?
That's a window.
There are many windows
in the house.

What's this?
It's a roof.
The roof is on top of the house.

Extra Dialogue

Yukio: Thanks for the invitation.
Donald: Be sure to come, and bring Hiromi.
Yukio: What's your address?
Donald: We live at seven-twenty-one Brandeis Street.
Yukio: That's hard to pronounce.
Donald: Let me spell it for you, B-r-a-n-d-e-i-s.
Yukio: I've got it.
Donald: See you Saturday at 7:00 p.m.
Yukio: Thanks again. See you next Saturday.

Answer the Questions
1. Who's inviting Yukio?
2. Where does Donald live?
3. Is the name of the street easy to pronounce?
4. Do you know how to spell the name of the street?
5. At which time is Yukio invited to Donald's home?
6. For which day is Yukio invited to Donald's home?

Copy

bedroom _____ kitchen _____ next to _____

The kitchen is next to the bedroom. _____

trees _____ in front of _____

There are trees in front of the house. _____

pretty _____ flowers _____

There are pretty flowers. _____

cat _____ on top of _____

The cat is on top of the car. _____

Pronunciation Practice

Words

bathroom	a bathroom	bathrooms
bedroom	a bedroom	bedrooms
downstairs	upstairs	anytime
address	an address	addresses
garage	a garage	garages
shade	wash	watch
mean	meal	keep
welcome	wonderful	invitation
where	who	what
when	why	how

Questions

What's that?

Where do you live?

How many bedrooms are there?

Where is one bedroom?

How many bathrooms are there?

Where is one bathroom?

Statements

That's our home.

We live here.

There are three bedrooms.

One bedroom is on the first floor.

There are two bathrooms.

One bathroom is downstairs.

Where is the other bathroom?	The other bathroom is upstairs.
Where is the garage?	The garage is next to the house.
Where is the extra room?	There is an extra room on top of the garage.
Where are the trees?	There are trees in front of the house.
Where are the flowers?	The flowers are in front of the house.
How are the flowers?	The flowers are pretty.

Questions	*Answers*
This is your home, isn't it?	Yes, it is. It's our home.
Do you like it there?	Yes, we do. We like it there.
You like it there, don't you?	Yes, we do. We like it there.
	No, we don't. We don't like it there.
Are there three bedrooms in the house?	Yes, there are three bedrooms in the house.
Is there a bedroom on the first floor?	Yes, there's a bedroom on the first floor.
There's a bedroom on the second floor, isn't there?	No, there are two bedrooms on the second floor.
There are three bathrooms, aren't there?	No, there are two bathrooms.
Is there a bathroom downstairs?	Yes, there's a bathroom downstairs.
There's a bathroom upstairs, isn't there?	Yes, there's a bathroom upstairs.
Is there a family room?	Yes, we have a family room.
You have a garage, don't you?	Yes, we have a garage.
Is there an extra room?	Yes, there's an extra room.
There's an extra garage, isn't there?	No, there's no extra garage.
Are there any trees?	Yes, there are trees.
There aren't any pretty flowers, are there?	Yes, there are some pretty flowers.
	No, there aren't any pretty flowers there.

Use of **wh Questions:** *how/who/which/where/what/when/why*

Extra Dialogue

Hiromi:	*How* are you today, José?
José:	Fine, thanks.
Hiromi:	*Who's* that man over there?
José:	*Which* man?
Hiromi:	I mean the one in the red coat.
José:	*Where's* a man in a red coat?
Hiromi:	He's standing next to my friend Manuel.
José:	Oh! That man? That's Ron Plaza.
Hiromi:	*What* does he do?
José:	He's an electrician.
Hiromi:	That's wonderful. *When* does he work?
José:	Monday through Friday from 8 a.m. to 5 p.m.
Hiromi:	*Where* does he work?
José:	*Why* do you ask?
Hiromi:	Because I need an electrician.
José:	His phone number is PLaza 2-8430.

Answer the Questions
1. How's José?
2. Who is with José?
3. Who's the man in the red coat?
4. What does Ron Plaza do?
5. Why does Hiromi need Ron's phone number?
6. What's Ron's phone number?

Repeat

Questions	Answers
How's our home?	It's beautiful.
How's Grandmother?	She's fine.
Who's at the party?	The family is at the party.
Who gives Grandmother presents?	We give Grandmother presents.

Which present do you like?	I like all presents.
Which bedroom is on the first floor?	My bedroom is on the first floor.
Where are the other bedrooms?	The other two bedrooms are on the second floor.
Where is one bathroom?	It's downstairs.
What's upstairs?	There's a bathroom upstairs.
What's on top of the garage?	There's an extra room there.
When do you go to class?	I go to class every day.
When does the family get together?	The family gets together each year.
Why does the family get together?	They get together for Grandmother's birthday.
Why do we sing "Happy Birthday?"	We sing "Happy Birthday" on Grandmother's birthday.

Positions

above/below/under/on top of/in front of/next to/beside

There is an extra room *above* the garage.
Below the extra room is the garage.
Your book's *under* the chair.
On top of the desk are Grandmother's presents.
There are many trees *in front of* the house.
Next to the chair stands the piano.
Beside the piano are some book shelves.

Where's the extra room?	It's *above* the garage.
Where's the garage?	It's *below* the extra room.
Where's the book?	The book is *under* the chair.
Where are the presents?	They are *on top of* the desk.
Where are the trees?	The trees are *in front of* the house.
Where's the piano?	It stands *next to* the chair.
Where are the book shelves?	They're *beside* the piano.

Practice

Change the following statements to questions. Use the question words in parentheses.

> **Example:** There are many presents. (where)
> <u>Where</u> are the presents?

1. He likes to sit on the sofa. (where)

_____

2. Ron works from 8 a.m. to 5 p.m. (when)

_____

3. Hiromi reads quickly. (how)

_____

4. Mrs. Carson is a good doctor. (who)

_____

5. He likes the small sofa. (which)

_____

6. Today we have a birthday party. (why)

_____

Substitution Drill

1. Hiromi is in the **bedroom.**
   bathroom.
   kitchen.
   living room.

2. There are some books **under** the chair.
   next to
   beside
   on top of

3. There are **two bedrooms** in our house.

       two bathrooms

       many chairs

       two people

4. We have a room **above** the garage.

          next to

          behind

          beside

5. The basket is **under** the table.

        on top of

        next to

        beside

Study

Use of a/an/the/some
Review:
Some nouns are *counted.* We call them *count nouns. A/an/the* is used with words that are *one* or *many.*

    Examples: Hiromi sits on <u>a chair.</u>

              She's eating <u>an apple.</u>   one

              <u>The apple</u> tastes good.

      There are <u>many chairs</u> in the room.

      She's buying <u>many apples.</u>

      <u>Some apples</u> are better than others.   many

      There are <u>six homes</u> on this street.

      <u>Our homes</u> are comfortable.

Some nouns are not *counted.* They're called *non-count nouns* or *mass nouns.*

Examples:

	count nouns	mass nouns
	one many	only one form
(the) a plate	some plates	some money
(the) a chair	some chairs	some milk
(the) a garage	some garages	some sugar
(the) a drink	some drinks	some coffee
(the) a pencil	some pencils	some chalk

Examples:

Hiromi likes milk.	—Give me <u>some</u> milk.
The tea is hot.	—Bring her <u>some</u> hot tea.
Money is important.	—José has <u>some</u> money.
He does not like sugar.	—Please pass me <u>some</u> (*the*) sugar.

Use of Count *Nouns or* Mass *Nouns*

What's on the table?
There's a cup on the table.

What's on the table?
There are some cups on the table.
There are three cups on the table.

What's on the table?
There is some fruit on the table.

What's on the plate?
There's a vegetable on a plate.

What's on the plate?
There are some vegetables on the plate.
There are four different
vegetables on the plate.

What's in the cup?
There's some tea in the cup.

What's on the plate?
There's a spoon on the plate.

What's on the plate?
There are three spoons on the plate.
There are some spoons on the plate.

What's in the cup?
There's some coffee
in the cup.

What's on the desk?
There's a pencil on the desk.

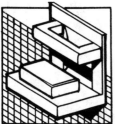

What's in the bathroom?
There's some soap in the bathroom.

What's on the desk?
There are some
pencils on the desk.
There are five pencils on the desk.

What's on the chair?
There's some money on the chair.

What's in the drawer?
There's some chalk in the drawer.

What's on the desk?
There's a book on the desk.

What's on the desk?
There are some
books on the desk.
There are four books
on the desk.

What's on the table?
There's some cream on the table.
There's some milk on the table.
There's some sugar on the table.

Copy—Special Expressions

a cup of tea	_____
a dish of food	_____
a drink of juice	_____
a drop of water	_____
a glass of milk	_____
a piece of cake	_____

Study

Comparison of Adjectives and Adverbs

This is a *small* desk.	His desk is *smaller* than mine.
That's a *big* car.	My car is *bigger* than yours.
Donald runs *fast*.	Mike runs *faster* than Donald.
Hiromi is a *quick* reader.	Henry is a *quicker* reader than Hiromi.
He reads *quickly*.	I read *more quickly* than he does.
I study *carefully*.	Ann studies *more carefully* than I.

Practice

Fill in the ADJECTIVE or the ADVERB using the word in parentheses.

Example: Hiromi learns quickly. (quick)

1. You drive _____ . (fast)

2. José always reads _____ . (quick)

3. These apples are _____ . (expensive)

4. Ann talks _____ . (fast)

5. I understand _____ . (easy)

6. This lesson is _____ . (easy)

7. Victoria writes _____ . (careless)

8. His car is _____ . (beautiful)

9. Mr. Powell speaks _____ . (beautiful)

10. Dr. Carson gets up _____ . (early)

Study

Review *of Adjective Comparison*
Our street is *busy*.
Their street is *busier* than ours.
Your street is not *as busy as* theirs.

Going to college is *expensive.*
Going on a trip is *more expensive.*
Staying home is *less expensive than* taking a trip.
Staying home is not *as expensive as* taking a trip.

Our book is *easy.* Theirs is also *easy.*
Our book is *easier than* theirs.
Their book is *as easy as* ours.
Our books are about *the same.*

Lisa is *tall.* She is *taller than* José.
José is not *as tall as* Isaac. Ron is *shorter than* Lisa.
Ron is very *short.*

Mr. Naga is *old.* He's *older than* Mr. Carson.
Mr. Naga is *as old as* Mrs. Naga.
Mrs. Naga is the *same* age *as* Mr. Naga.

My book is *heavy.* Ron's book is *as heavy as* mine. Angel's book is
heavier than ours. It's not *heavier than* Ann's.

Review *of Adverb Comparison*

He talks *fast.* I talk *faster than* he does.
She doesn't talk *as fast as* I do.

I learn *easily.* Ann learns more *easily than* I do.
Mike learns *as easily as* I do.

We drive *carefully.* Our neighbors drive *as carefully as* we do.
They don't drive *more carefully than* we do.

José always reads *quickly.* He reads more *quickly than* Ann.
But he doesn't read *as quickly as* Harry.

Practice

Positions

Make *questions*. Begin each question with the word *where*.

> **Example:** The chairs are in the living room.
> <u>Where</u> are the chairs?

1. We're in the living room.

   _____

2. The family is in the kitchen.

   _____

3. Hiromi puts forks on the table.

   _____

4. The book is under the desk.

   _____

5. The lamp is above the door.

   _____

6. The garage is below the room.

   _____

7. The trees are in front of the house.

   _____

8. José's room is on top of the garage.

   _____

9. Ann stands behind Hiromi.

   _____

10. Mr. Naga stands beside Mrs. Carson.

    _____

11. The flowers are next to the house.

    _____

What Do You See?

You're in the *living room*.
What do you see? *Where* do you see it?

I see a couch.
The couch stands in the corner.

I see some chairs.
The chairs are in front of the couch.

I see a piano.
The piano stands
beside the wall.

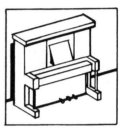

I see book shelves.
The book shelves are on the wall.

I see a fireplace.
The fireplace is next
to the piano.

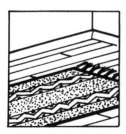

I see a carpet.
The carpet is on the floor.

I see a picture.
The picture hangs
on the wall.
It hangs above the couch.

I see the piano stool.
The stool stands in front of the piano.

What's There?

Use *a/number/some*

Examples:

What's on the desk?
There's <u>a book</u> on the desk.

What's on the desk?
There are <u>three books</u> on the desk.
There are <u>some books</u> on the desk.

What's on the table?
There's _____ on the table.

What's on the table?
There are _____ on the table.
There are _____ on the table.

What's in the drawer?

There's _____ chalk in the drawer.

What's on the plate?

There's _____ on the plate.

What's in the bowl?

There's _____ fruit in the bowl.

What's in the cup?

There's _____ tea in the cup.

What's in the bottle?

There's _____ milk in the bottle.

What's on the plate?

There's _____ spoon on the plate.

What's on the table?

There are _____ spoons on the table.

There are _____ spoons on the table.

What's in the cup?

There's _____ coffee in the cup.

What's on the desk?

There's _____ pencil on the desk.

What's on the desk?

There are _____ pencils on the desk.

There are _____ pencils on the desk.

What's under the chair?

There's _____ money under the chair.

What's beside the desk?

There's _____ beside the desk.

What's in front of the garage?

There's _____ car in front of the garage.

What's in front of the garage?

There are _____ cars in front of the garage.

There are _____ cars in front of the garage.

What's on the table?

There's _____ cream on the table.

There's _____ milk on the table.

There's _____ sugar on the table.

What's above the table?

There's _____ lamp above the table.

Where Are You?

Example:

You're driving.
<u>I'm in a car.</u>

You're sleeping.

I'm in _____ .

You're eating dinner.

I'm _____ .

You're watching TV.

I'm _____ .

You're cooking dinner.

I'm _____ .

You're studying your lesson.

I'm _____ .

You're taking out a book.

I'm _____ .

You're riding to school.

I'm _____ .

You're talking with your friends.

I'm _____ .

You're taking an exam.

I'm _____ .

Extra Dialogue

What's under your arm?

Uh, nothing.

It isn't nothing. Is it a book?

No, they're some magazines.

What kind are they?

They're sports magazines.

Lend me one, please.

O.K. But return it soon!

Copy

what _____ under _____ arm _____

What's under your arm? _____

they're _____ some _____ magazines

They're some magazines. _____

kind _____ sports _____ lend _____

What kind are they? _____

They're sports magazines. _____

Lend me one, please. _____

return _____ soon _____ please _____

O.K. But return it soon. _____

Substitution Drill

1. Thank you for the **apples**.
                    fruit.
                    milk.
                    coffee.

2. Please send him a **book**.
                    letter.
                    present.
                    message.

3. She's having some **coffee**.
                    tea.
                    milk.
                    fruit.

4. Hiromi is ordering some **toast**.
                    milk.
                    tea.
                    coffee.

5. The teacher is looking for some **chalk**.
                    books.
                    students.
                    chairs.

Exercises

Use a *or* some

Example: Please give me <u>some</u> milk.

1. Hiromi has _____ book.

2. Ann buys _____ pen.

3. There are _____ pencils on the desk.

4. There's _____ soap in the bathroom.

5. Mike asks for _____ toothpaste.

6. There are _____ chairs in the corner.

7. I see _____ sofa under the picture.

8. The child plays on _____ carpet.

9. They're buying _____ carpets.

10. He's standing under _____ tree.

11. There's _____ cup on the table.

12. Let's go and buy _____ milk.

13. Don't you have _____ dish for the potatoes?

14. Why don't you put _____ milk on the table?

15. Ann puts _____ cream into the coffee.

16. The waitress gives Hiromi _____ check.

17. The old lady buys _____ green vegetables.

18. The living room has _____ pretty carpets.

19. We have _____ good TV set.

Use a, an *or* a piece of

Example: Mike has <u>an</u> apple.

1. He's looking for _____ toothbrush.

2. Please give me _____ fruit.

3. Ann eats _____ bread.

4. Mr. Powell needs _____ chalk.

5. José eats _____ orange.

6. Bring me _____ vegetable, please.

7. She doesn't have _____ pen.

8. Manuel likes _____ cold drink.

9. Isaac needs _____ invitation.

10. Victoria reads _____ magazine.

11. Give me _____ toast.

12. Write me _____ letter, please.

Use Special Expressions *with* Mass *Nouns*

Example: Ann orders <u>a cup of</u> tea. (cup)

1. Please bring me _____ coffee. (cup)

2. She orders _____ tea. (cup)

3. Mike asks for _____ food. (dish)

4. Grandmother cuts _____ cake. (piece)

5. Hiromi drinks _____ milk. (glass)

6. Don't worry, it's only _____ water. (drop)

7. Manuel enjoys _____ water. (drink)

Puzzle

ALL OF these things are in a house.
Fill in the missing letters.

Across

1. You sit on it.
2. You open it and walk into a room.
3. You keep a car in it.
4. You cook in it.

Down

5. You play music on it.
6. You sleep in it.
7. You wash up in it.
8. You write on it.

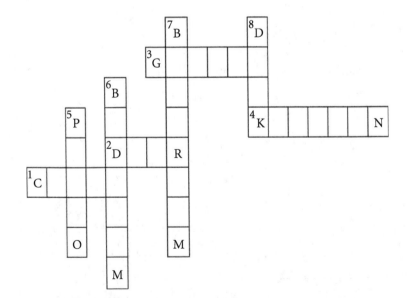

Unscramble

Unscramble the letters to make words.

Example: veboa = <u>above</u>

lobew _____   nihebd _____

rednu _____   mose _____

tnex _____   uoseh _____

norft _____   seetr _____

desieb _____   nowd _____

Answers to Unscramble:

below; under; next; front; beside; behind; some; house; trees; down

Completion

Complete the talk using the words below.

> in front of   next   wonderful   above   extra   bathroom

Mike: What's _____ the garage?

Angel: Oh, that's an _____ room.

Manuel: An extra room? That's _____ !

Lisa: What's _____ to the room?

Angel: It's my _____ .

Mike: Your bathroom? How about a car?

Angel: My car's _____ _____ _____ the garage.

Complete the reading using the words below.

> downstairs   on top of   bedrooms   on   upstairs
> in front of   next to

There are three _____ in our house. One bedroom is _____ the first floor. One bathroom is _____ . Another bathroom is _____ . The garage is _____ the house. There is an extra room _____ the garage. There are some trees _____ the house.

Listen and Write

This is our home.   _____

It is beautiful.   _____

We live here.   _____

There are two bedrooms.   _____

There is a family room.   _____

We cook in the kitchen.   _____

The garage is beside the house. _____

There are some trees in front. _____

There are many flowers.   _____

Write a situation about the following dialogue.

Dan:	We have a beautiful home.
Gloria:	Yes, let's invite some people.
Ann:	Good idea. Let's have a party.
Hiromi:	I'm calling Manuel already.
Dan:	Not so fast.
Gloria:	Hold it, Hiromi.
Ann:	Let's plan the party first.

Write a dialogue about the following situation.

You're watching TV.
Your father calls.
He asks you to help in the kitchen.
You don't like to walk away from the TV.
Your father calls again angrily.
You say O.K.
He thanks you.

Proverb

There is no place like home. (No matter where you are, it's not like being at home with your family.)

CHAPTER TEN

Our Town

IN THIS CHAPTER

Directions: *right/left/straight ahead/around the corner/ opposite/follow/block/across*

Review the Use of *in/on/at* with *time/* and *place*

Adjectives and Adverbs Comparisons

Use of *alike/different/the same/similar*

Use of *turn on/turn off*

A Plan of our City

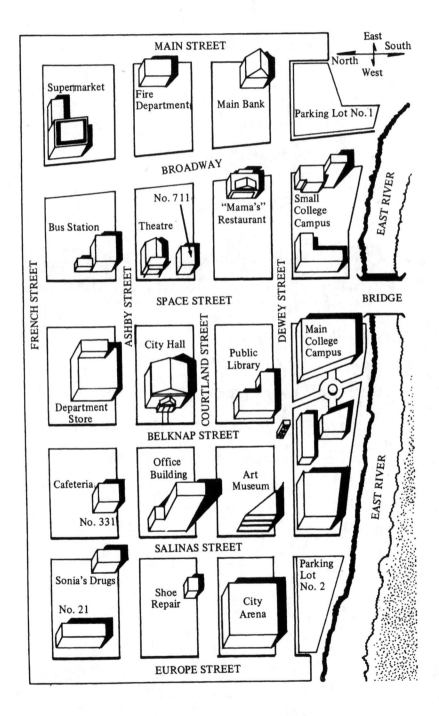

Read

Situation

This is our town. It is a small town, but we like it here. We live at 711 Space Street. Out friends live at 21 Europe Street. Their street is across town. There is a theater around the corner. Down the street is a bus station, and two blocks away is our fire department. There is a college campus nearby. During the rush hour the traffic is heavy. We often eat at Mama's Restaurant on Broadway.

Listen/Talk

Dialogue

Jenny: I'm looking for Europe Street.

Hiromi: We're on Main and Ashby.

Ann: What number on Europe Street?

Jenny: 21.

Ann: Oh, that's easy.

Jenny: I'm looking for my friends, the Powells.

Ann: I know where the Powells live.

Jenny: Show me, please.

Ann: Go two blocks to Dewey Street.

Jenny: O.K. Then what?

Ann: Turn right on Dewey, then go five blocks and turn right again.

Jenny: Where's number 21?

Ann: It's on the corner of Ashby and Europe.

Jenny: Thanks. Where do you live?

Ann: I live at 711 Space Street. It's almost around the corner from the Powells.

Answer the Questions

1. What street is Jenny looking for?
2. What number is it?
3. Who lives there?
4. Where is 21 Europe Street?
5. Where does Ann live?

Copy

town _____ This is our town. _____

small _____ It is a small town. _____

live _____ We live on Space Street. _____

our _____ friends _____ Europe _____ street _____

Our friends live on Europe Street. _____

across _____ around _____ corner _____ blocks _____

away _____ fire _____ department _____

They live across town. _____

There is a theater around the corner. _____

Two blocks away is the fire department. _____

nearby _____ college _____ campus _____

There is a college campus nearby. _____

during _____ rush _____ heavy _____ traffic _____

The traffic is heavy during rush hour. _____

Repeat—Where Are We

This is Parking Lot number 1.
We're on the corner of Main and Dewey.

That's the fire department.
We're on Main and Ashby.

This is the theater.
We're on Space and Ashby.

That's 711 Space Street.
We're in the Carson home.

This is the bus station.
We're on Ashby and Space.

That's the college campus.
We're on Dewey Street.

This is a traffic light.
We're at the intersection of Belknap and Dewey.

This is Mama's Restaurant.
We're on Broadway.

That's the shoe store.
We're on Courtland.

This is the main bank.
We're on Main
and Dewey.

That's the public library.
We're on Belknap
and Dewey.

This is the art museum.
We're on Salinas and Dewey.

That's Sonia's Drugs.
We're on Salinas
and Ashby.

Extra Dialogue

Lisa: I'm looking for the public library.
Ron: It isn't far from here. We're on French and Main.
Lisa: How do I get there?
Ron: Go to the intersection of Broadway and Dewey.
Lisa: And then?
Ron: Take a right on Dewey. Go to the traffic light on Belknap
and Dewey.
Lisa: Is the library on the corner of Belknap and Dewey?
Ron: That's where it is.

Answer the Questions

1. What is Lisa asking for?
2. Is she far from the library?
3. Where does Lisa have to go?
4. Where is the library?

Copy

looking _____ public _____ library _____

I'm looking for the public library. _____

intersection _____ far _____ here _____

Go to the intersection. _____

It isn't far from here. _____

traffic _____ light _____ there _____

There is a traffic light. _____

The library is on the corner. _____

Pronunciation Practice

Words

| library | a library | the library | libraries |

I am looking for the public library.

| town | a town | the town | towns |

This is our town.

| corner | a corner | the corner | corners |

Around the corner is the theater.

| station | a station | the station | stations |

Down the street is a bus station.

| block | a block | the block | blocks |

Two blocks away is the fire department.

| campus | a campus | the campus | campuses |

There is a college campus nearby.

| restaurant | a restaurant | the restaurant | restaurants |

We often eat at Mama's Restaurant.

Questions	Statements
What's this?	This is our town.
Where do we live?	We live in a small town.
Why do we live here?	We like it here.
What address is this?	This is 711 Space Street.
Where do your friends live?	Our friends live on Europe Street.
Where is Europe Street?	Europe Street is across town.
What's around the corner?	There's a theater around the corner.
Where's the bus station?	The bus station is down the street.
Where's the fire department?	The fire department is two blocks away.
Where's the college campus?	The college campus is nearby.
When is the traffic heavy?	The traffic is heavy during rush hour.
Where do we often eat?	We eat at Mama's Restaurant.
Where is the restaurant?	The restaurant is on Broadway.

Questions	Answers
This is your town, isn't it?	Yes, it's our town.
You like it here, don't you?	Yes, we do. We like it here.
Do you live in a small town?	Yes, we live in a small town.
Do you live in a big town?	No, we don't. We live in a small town.
Is this 711 Space Street?	Yes, this is 711 Space Street.
Your friends live on Europe Street, don't they?	Yes, they do.
Europe Street is one block down, isn't it?	No, it isn't. It's across town.
Isn't there a theater around the corner?	Yes, there is a theater around the corner.
The bus station is down the street, isn't it?	Yes, the bus station is down the street.
Is the fire department two blocks away?	Yes, the fire department is two blocks away.
There is a college campus nearby, isn't there?	Yes, there is a college campus nearby.
Isn't the traffic heavy during rush hour?	Yes, the traffic is heavy during rush hour.

We often eat at Mama's Restaurant, don't we?	Yes, we do.
The restaurant is on Belknap Street, isn't it?	No, it isn't. It's on Broadway.

Pattern Practice

1. town
   a small town
   We live in a small town.

2. like it
   we like it
   We like it here.

3. street
   their street
   Their street is across town.

4. corner
   around the corner
   We live around the corner.

5. theater
   there is a theater
   There is a theater around the corner.

6. bus
   a bus station
   Down the street is a bus station.

7. campus
   a college campus
   There is a college campus nearby.

8. traffic
   heavy traffic
   The traffic is heavy.

9. restaurant
   we often eat at Mama's
   We often eat at Mama's Restaurant.

10. opposite
    the public library
    The public library is opposite our house.

11. department store
    there's nearby
    There's a department store nearby.

12. straight ahead
    then turn left
    Go straight ahead then turn left.

Substitution Drill

1. Where do you **live?**
   eat?
   study?
   read?

2. Where does **Mike** live?
   Hiromi
   Manuel
   Ann

3. I live in a small **town.**
   city.
   house.

4. He lives at **seven-eleven** Space Street.
   twenty-five
   forty-three
   sixty-seven

5. They live on **Space Street.**
   Broadway.
   Dewey Street.
   Belknap.

6. Do you live at **twenty-one** West Europe Street?
   thirty-three
   fifty-four
   seventy-nine

7. How far is it to **Broadway?**
   the fire department?
   the main bank?
   the town library?

8. Does Manuel live in **Peru?**
   Venezuela?
   New York?
   the U.S.A.?

9. Are you going to the **library?**
   bank?
   campus?
   restaurant?

10. The **restaurant** is around the corner.
    fire department
    campus
    library

Study—Prepositions

in (with time)—We say:
Question: *when*

1. *in* the morning; *in* the afternoon; *in* the evening; *in* a minute; *in* an hour; *in* a short time; *in* the nick of time
2. All of the months of the year
   Example: *in* May; *in* June; etc.
3. Any year
   Example: *in* 1979; *in* 1980
4. Any season
   Example: *in* the spring; *in* the summer; etc.

in (with place)—We say:
Question: *where*

1. *in* a small town; *in* a classroom; *in* the kitchen; *in* the car; etc.

on (with time)—We say:
Question: *when*

1. Any day of the week
   Example: *on* Monday; *on* Thursday; etc.
2. Any day of the month
   Example: *on* the fifth of March; *on* the second of the month; etc.
3. be *on* time

on (place)—We say:
Question: *where*

1. *on* the right; *on* the left; *on* the corner; *on* the same block; *on* our street; etc.
2. *on* the desk; *on* the wall; *on* the floor; etc.

at (time)—We say:
Question: *when*

1. Any hour
   Example: *at* five o'clock; *at* 3:00 p.m.; etc.
2. Any period of the day
   Example: *at* noon; *at* night; *at* midnight

at (place)—We say:
Question: *where*

1. *at* our place; *at* seven-eleven Space Street; *at* the Powells'; etc.

Practice

Prepositions

Select the correct *preposition* to complete the dialogue.

at   in   on

Where is Hiromi?

She's _____ her class.

_____ what time does she go home?

She's _____ home _____ noon.

When does she get up _____ the morning?

She gets up _____ 8:00 a.m.

O.K. See you _____ an hour.

'Bye.

Fill in *at/in/on*

1. Hiromi is _____ her car.

2. The family is _____ the living room.

3. We live _____ 711 Space Street.

4. The teacher writes _____ the board.

5. There is a book _____ the floor.

6. We go to class _____ the morning.

7. Please write your lesson _____ your paper.

8. Don't write _____ your book.

9. The English class is _____ room 913.

10. They live _____ New York.

11. I have an appointment _____ 12 noon.

12. How many forks are _____ the table?

13. Sorry, José's not _____ school today.

14. Don't worry, the children are _____ home already.

15. Children are playing _____ the street.

What's Happening?

You're at some place . . . what's happening?

You're on the corner of French and Broadway.

What are you doing there?

We're _____ .

This is the corner of Ashby and Main.

What do we have here?

We have _____ .

This is the corner of Space and Ashby.

What do we see here?

We see _____ .

We're at seven-eleven Space Street.

Who lives here?

_____ .

You're on Belknap and Dewey.

What are you doing here?

We _____ .

This is Main and Dewey.
What do we see here?

We _____ .

We're at twenty-one
Europe Street.
Who lives here?

_____ .

We're now in the block of Space,
Dewey, and Salinas.
What do we have here?

We have _____ .

You are now on the corner of
Dewey and Salinas.
Where are you now?
We are _____ .

We're in the block of
Ashby, Salinas,
Belknap, and Courtland.
What are we doing here?

We're _____ .

We're at 331 Ashby.
What's there?
It's the . . . _____ .

Study

Review—Adjectives

1. Ask how *many?*

How many chairs are there?	There are *fifteen* chairs in the room.
How many students are here?	There are *thirty* students here.
How many books do you have?	I have *one hundred* books.

2. Ask *what kind?*

What kind of jacket is this?	This is a *summer* jacket.
What kind of dress is that?	That's a *winter* dress.
What kind of lesson is this?	It's an *English* lesson.

3. Ask *which one?*

   There are three cars in the garage. *Which one* is yours?
   The *beautiful* one is mine.

   I like this class. *Which one* don't you like?
   I don't like the *difficult* class.

   Which one of those houses is yours?
   The *big* one is ours.

Adverbs

Adverbs ask *how/when/where/in what way (manner)/under what conditions*

1. Ask *how?*

How are you?	I'm *fine*, thank you.
How does Ann run?	She runs *quickly*.
How does Hiromi study?	She studies *slowly*.
How do they work?	They work *gladly*.
How does she write?	She writes *beautifully*.

2. Ask *when?*

When do you eat lunch?	I eat lunch *before* noon.
When do they study?	They study *often*.

When do they work?	They work *nights* and sleep *days.*
When does he listen?	He *seldom* listens.
When do you play?	I play *Saturdays.*

3. Ask *where?*

Where is he going?	He is going *away.*
Where are they?	They're *here.*
Where is the car?	The car is *outside.*
Where is the restaurant?	It's to the *left* of the library.
Where is the campus?	The campus is *straight* ahead.

Practice

Fill in the correct form of the ADJECTIVE or ADVERB.

Example: She walks very <u>slowly.</u> (slow)

He is a <u>slow</u> (slow) reader.

1. Mike learns _____ . (quick)

2. Ann is a _____ driver. (fast)

3. Manuel learns _____ . (fast)

4. This lesson is _____ . (easy)

5. We speak _____ . (correct)

6. This story is _____ . (correct)

7. Lisa is never _____ to study. (glad)

8. Alice studies _____ . (glad)

9. The teacher prepares the lesson _____ . (careless)

Study

Review—Comparative

1. One-syllable adjectives add *-er* to form comparatives.

This is a *short* book.	This book is *shorter* than that one.
My class is *small.*	Hiromi's class is *smaller* than mine.
Ann's desk is *long.*	Mike's desk is *longer* than Ann's.
Hiromi's mother is *old.*	Manuel's mother is *older* than Hiromi's.

2. Some adjectives form *irregular* comparatives.

Manuel is a *good* secretary.   Some secretaries are *better* than Manuel.

I have a *bad* headache.   My headache is *worse* than yours.

3. Longer adjectives require *more* or *less* to form comparatives.

Our class is *more interesting* than yours.

My girlfriend is *more beautiful* than his.

This lesson is *less difficult* than that one.

Please be *more polite* when you drive.

This book is *less expensive* than that one.

Sometimes things *are* or *aren't*

the same as

similar to

like   -other things

different from

Pattern Drill

All patterns below are in the *singular*. To form the *plural* patterns change *is* to *are, isn't* to *aren't,*

> **Example:** My chair <u>is</u> the same as his.
> Our chairs <u>are</u> the same as theirs.

1. *Affirmative*

His coat		the same as	mine.
That desk	is	similar to	this one.
This girl		like	my sister.
Our class		different from	theirs.

2. *Negative*

Hiromi's exam		the same as	José's.
Ann's car	is not	similar to	mine.
Lisa's dress	isn't	like	her mother's.
Their exam		different from	ours.

3. *Affirmative Question*

IS	your book	the same as	that one?
	her car	similar to	this one?
	their house	like	ours?
	that building	different from	the one on Main Street?

4. *Negative Question*

ISN'T	my hat	the same as	Manuel's?
	her coat	similar to	Ann's?
	his house	like	mine?
	their campus	different from	ours?

Practice

1. My car is *as good as* yours.
2. His desk is *as long as* Ann's.
3. My mother is *as old as* her mother.
4. Hiromi and Ann don't *look alike.*
5. José and Manuel *look alike.*
6. Our coats *look alike.*
7. Aren't our customs *different?*
8. Isn't his house *different* from mine?
9. Make all of your sentences *different.*
10. Every person is *different.*

Fill in the correct form of the *Comparative*

Example: This lesson is <u>easier</u> than the last one. (easy)

Their house is <u>more beautiful</u> than ours. (beautiful)

1. Our campus is _____ than theirs. (big)
2. The traffic is _____ during rush hours. (heavy)
3. Their street is _____ than ours. (wide)

4. Ann studies _____ than Hiromi. (fast)

5. José drives _____ than Angel. (slow)

6. Aaron is _____ than his brother. (small)

7. This man is _____ than that one. (thin)

8. My parents drive _____ than I do. (fast)

9. This is a _____ town than New York. (small)

10. His country is _____ than mine. (big)

Extra Dialogue

Mr. Carson:	It's dark in here. Please turn on the light.
Hiromi:	Let's listen to some music. Turn on the radio.
Ann:	I'm going to sleep. Turn off the radio, please.
Hiromi:	Wait. Let's turn on the TV and watch one program.
Ann:	I'm too tired. Turn it off, please.
Hiromi:	O.K., O.K. Let's turn off everything.

Answer the Questions

1. Why does Hiromi turn on the light?
2. What else does Hiromi turn on?
3. Why does Ann tell Hiromi to turn off the radio?
4. What does Hiromi like to turn on?
5. Why is Ann going to sleep?

Practice

How Do You Get There?

You are in the supermarket on Broadway and W. French Street.
How do you get to Mama's Restaurant?

_____

There's a fire at 21 Europe Street.
How does the fire department get there?

_____

You're at the city arena.
How do you get to
the bus station?

_____

You're on the main campus.
How do you get to our friend's
home at 21 Europe Street?

_____

We're at 711 Space Street.
How do we get to 21 Europe?

_____

We're at the City Hall.
How do we get to Mama's Restaurant?

_____

We're at Mama's Restaurant.
How do we get to the main bank?

_____

You're at the main bank.
How do you get to the supermarket?

_____

You're at the office building.
How do you get to the main campus?

_____

We're at Sonia's Drugs.
How do we get to the
East River Bridge?

_____

You're at 711 Space Street.
How do you get to the city arena?

_____

They're at 21 Europe.
How do they get to the small campus?

_____

You're at the department store.
How do you get to Mama's Restaurant?

_____

You're at the supermarket.
How do you get to the East River?

_____

We're at the theater.
How do we get to the shoe store?

_____

We're at Parking Lot number 1.
How do we get to the city arena?

_____

They're at Sonia's Drugs.
How do they get to City Hall?

_____

We're at the art museum.
How do we get to the theater?

_____

You're at the bus station.
How do you get to the cafeteria?

_____

What Are You Doing There?

Example: You're at the supermarket.
What are you doing there?
<u>I'm buying groceries.</u>

You're at 21 Europe Street.
What are you doing there?

_____

You're on the college campus.
What are you doing there?

_____

We're at 711 Space Street.
What are we doing here?

They're at Mama's Restaurant.
What are they doing there?

_____

You're at the main bank.
What are you doing there?

_____

They're in the
office building.
What are they doing there?

_____

That's a department store.
What are they selling there?

_____

We're at Sonia's Drugs.
What are we buying there?

_____

They're at the theater.
What are they seeing there?

_____

You're at Parking Lot number 1.
What are you doing there?

_____

_____

We're at the bus station.
What are we taking there?

_____

Change Statements to Questions

Change the sentences below to *questions*. Use the question word in parentheses.

> **Example:** The family is in the living room. (where)
> <u>Where is the family?</u>

1. We live in a small town. (where)

_____

2. The Powells live at 21 Europe Street. (where)

_____

3. Their street is across town. (where)

_____

4. The theater is around the corner. (what)

_____

5. Down the street is a bus station. (what)

_____

6. Two blocks away is the fire department. (where)

_____

7. We're buying groceries for dinner. (why)

_____

8. There is heavy traffic during the rush hour. (when)

_____

9. On Sundays we eat at Mama's Restaurant. (when)

_____

10. The family has a reunion each year. (when)

_____

11. We get together on Grandmother's birthday. (why)

_____

12. My brother likes to sit on the sofa. (where)

_____

13. They keep their car in the garage. (where)

_____

14. The supermarket is on French and Broadway. (where)

_____

15. The Carsons go shopping. (who)

_____

Use turn on/turn off

Example: There's too much noise here; <u>turn off</u> the radio.

1. It's daylight outside; _____ the light.
2. It's dark in the office; _____ the light.
3. It's freezing cold in the room; _____ the heat.
4. It's too hot in my study; _____ the heat.
5. I don't feel like reading; let's _____ the TV.
6. I have a test tomorrow; _____ the TV.

Puzzle

All of these words give *directions*. First write the word on the line. Then write it in the puzzle.

Across

1. It is on the _____ side of the street.

2. When you continue going _____ .

3. The theater is around the _____ .

Down

4. You _____ this street to the end.

5. The supermarket is _____ the corner.

6. Go _____ ahead.

7. Walk carefully _____ the street.

8. Don't go right; go _____ .

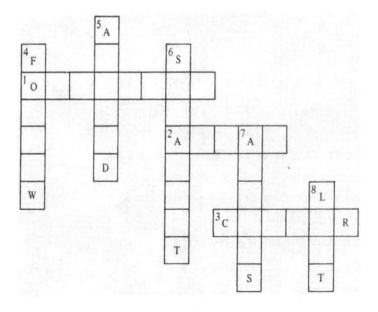

Unscramble

Unscramble the letters to make words.

Example: *crsosa* = <u>*across*</u>

hirgt _____	*clokb* _____
elft _____	*loflow* _____
haead _____	*kelia* _____
nuorad _____	*meas* _____
nercor _____	*lasimir* _____

Answers to Unscramble:

right; left; ahead; around; corner; block; follow; alike; same; similar

Completion

Complete the talk using the words below.

home   know   number   for   going   Street

Mike: I'm looking _____ Belknap Street.

Ron: What's the _____ ?

Mike: I don't _____ .

Ron: Where are you _____ ?

Mike: To the Powells' _____ .

Ron: Oh, I know where it is; it's 21 Europe _____ .

Talk about your hometown or city.

Tell us the name of your town or city.
Tell us what country you come from.
Tell us about the street on which you live.
Tell us about interesting things in your hometown.
Tell us how big the town is.
Tell us how many people live there.
Tell us about some people you know.
Tell us about your family.

Listen and Write

this _____ is _____ our _____ town _____

This is our town. _____

It _____ small _____ town _____

It is a small town. _____

we _____ like _____ here _____

We like it here. _____

theater _____ around _____ corner _____

The theater is around the corner. _____

nearby _____ college _____ campus _____

There is a college campus nearby. _____

often _____ eat _____ restaurant _____

We often eat at Mama's Restaurant. _____

Write a dialogue about the following situation.

You are driving a car.
You almost have an accident.
The policeman tells you to be careful.
You promise to drive carefully.
He tells you to watch the traffic lights.
You say that you will be careful.
He tells you to go on.
You thank him.

Write a situation about the following dialogue.

You really have a nice house.
Oh, I don't know.
Well, it's nicer than ours.
I don't think so.
In our town, houses are smaller.
I think they're the same as ours.
Really? It's nice of you to say so.

Proverb

If at first you don't succeed, try and try again.
(Some persons take a little longer to learn than others,
but that should not discourage them from continuing.)

Appendix

All words are listed in alphabetical order. The number following each word indicates the chapter where the word was first used.

about	4	aunt	8	bring	6
above	9	auto mechanic	2	brother	1
absent	4	autumn	5	brother-in-law	8
accident	10	back	7	brown	7
across	9	bag	7	brush	9
address	3	baker	7	bus	1
afraid	4	bakery	7	business	5
after	3	banana	7	but	6
afternoon	1	bank	10	butcher	7
again	8	basket	9	butter	7
agree	8	bathroom	9	buy	7
ahead	10	be	1	by	4
airport	6	bean	7	cafeteria	1
aisle	7	bear	5	call up	4
album	8	beautiful	5	call	4
alike	10	because	3	camel	5
alive	8	become	6	campus	10
almost	4	bedroom	9	car	2
already	9	beer	7	care	9
also	1	begin	1	careful	6
always	3	behind	4	carpet	9
American	2	below	9	carrot	7
and	1	bench	4	carton	7
angry	9	beside	9	cat	5
animal	5	bicycle	1	celebrate	8
another	2	big	5	celery	7
anytime	9	black	7	cereal	7
apple	7	block	10	certainly	6
are	1	blue	7	chair	4
arena	10	book	2	chalk	9
arm	6	bottle	9	change	2
around	3	bowl	9	cheap	7
arrival	4	boy	1	check	9
art	10	brake	3	cheese	7
ask	5	bread	7	chemistry	2
assignment	6	breakfast	3	chicken	7
at	4	bridge	10	city	6

class	1	direction	10	excellent	6
clock	3	discourage	10	expect	6
clothing	5	discover	8	expensive	7
coat	6	dish	9	experience	8
coffee	7	do	7	extra	
cold	5	doctor	2	eye	
come	1	dog	5	face	6
coming	3	door	9	fall	5
complain	6	dorm	4	family	8
continuation	6	down	6	far	10
continue	10	downstairs	9	farm	7
cookie	7	drawer	9	fast	8
cooking	7	dress	7	fat	6
cool	4	drink	2	father	1
copy	1	drive	8	feed	5
corn	7	driver	8	few	5
corner	7	driving	3	final	5
correct	8	drop	9	fine	1
cottage	7	dumb	6	finger	6
cousin	8	during	3	fire	10
cow	5	each	5	first	3
custom	10	ear	6	fish	7
cut	4	early	3	floor	4
cute	7	easy	5	flour	7
dark	10	egg	7	flower	9
date	5	elephant	5	follow	10
daughter	3	else	10	following	1
day	4	end	1	food	4
dear	6	english	2	foot	6
delicious	7	enjoy	5	forget	7
department	10	enough	4	fork	4
desert	5	europe	10	forks	4
desk	4	even	3	forward	8
dialogue	1	evening	1	freeze	6
different	10	every	7	French	2
difficult	5	everybody	4	fresh	7
dinner	3	examine	7	friend	1

from	1	hard	1	inside	4
front	9	harvest	5	interesting	5
fruit	7	hat	6	intersection	10
fun	6	have	1	introduce	2
gallon	7	he	1	invitation	9
garage	9	head	5	invite	4
garbage	7	hear	7	is	1
get in	1	heat	10	isle	7
get well	4	heavy	6	jacket	6
get	2	hello	1	japan	1
giraffe	5	help	4	jelly	7
girl	1	here	1	juice	7
give	8	himself	7	juicy	7
glad	2	history	3	keep	9
glass	4	hold it	9	kick	8
go	3	holiday	4	kind	5
good	1	home	2	kitchen	4
goodbye	1	honey	7	kleenex	7
gorilla	5	hope	6	knife	4
granddaughter	8	horse	5	knock	2
grandfather	8	hospital	2	know	5
grandmother	8	host	1	lab	1
grandson	8	hostess	1	lamp	9
great	3	hot dog	7	large	6
green	7	hot	5	last	3
greet	6	hour	3	late	3
grey	7	house	2	later	
grocery	7	how	1	lawyer	2
grow	5	hungry	1	learn	4
guess	1	hurry up	6	learner	8
guest	2	hurry	6	left	10
guide	1	husband	8	leg	6
hair	2	ice	6	lemon	7
half	7	idea	1	lend	9
hamburger	7	important	6	let's	2
hand	6	in front of	9	letter	6
hang	9	in	4	lettuce	7
happy	3	indeed		library	4

light	6	movies	3	on top	9
like	2	mr. = mister	1	onion	7
line	8	mrs. = miss	1	only	1
lion	5	much	2	opposite	10
lip	6	museum	10	or	6
list	7	music	8	orange	7
listen	1	my	1	order	9
little	1	name	1	other	9
live	2	napkin	4	out	3
loaf	7	narrow	6	outside	10
long	5	nearby	10	pants	6
look	4	neck	5	paper	7
lot	2	need	9	pardon	2
loud	6	nephew	8	parents	1
lower	7	never	3	party	1
magazine	9	new	5	pass	9
make	4	newspaper	2	paste	9
man	1	next to	9	patient	7
many	2	next	7	peanut	7
math	6	nice	8	pears	7
matter	8	nick	10	pen	3
meal	9	niece	8	pencil	3
mean	9	night	6	people	2
meat	4	noise	10	period	3
mechanic	2	nose	6	pet	5
meet	2	not	1	phone	4
message	9	notebook	4	piano	2
mexican	2	nothing	2	pick up	3
middle	7	now	1	pick	3
milk	5	nurse	2	picnic	8
mini	7	o'clock	3	pilot	6
minute	3	odd	3	place	4
money	6	office	4	plan	5
monkey	5	often	2	plant	5
month	6	oil	7	plate	4
morning	1	old	5	play	5
most	5	on time	3	player	2
mother	1	on top of	9	policeman	10

polite	10	reunion	8	sister	1
potato	7	ride	1	sister-in-law	8
pound	7	right	6	sit	5
preparation	4	ring	4	situation	1
prepare	4	ripe	7	sleep	3
present	8	rise	5	sleeping	3
pretty	7	river	10	sliced	7
previous	8	roof	9	slow	2
price	7	row	5	small	5
problem	6	run	8	snake	5
professor	2	runner	8	snow	6
program	10	rush	10	snows (it)	6
progress	2	sad	3	soap	7
promise	10	salesman	2	soccer	2
public	10	salt	7	sofa	9
put on	5	same as	10	some	9
put	5	same	10	sometimes	3
quick	8	school	1	soon	1
quite	4	season	5	sorry	4
rain	6	secretary	2	space	10
rains (it)	6	see	7	spoon	4
read	1	sell	2	sport	5
ready	4	semester	5	spring	5
real	7	send	6	stand	7
really	4	set	4	station	10
recorder	6	shade	9	stay	8
red	7	she	1	stool	9
registration	5	shelf	7	stop	3
relate	8	shirt	6	story	6
relation	8	shoe	6	straight ahead	10
relax	8	shop	2	street	10
remember	7	shopping	7	strong	5
repair	2	short	5	student	1
repeat	1	show	6	study	1
reporter	2	sick	3	studying	3
restaurant	1	similar to	10	stylist	2
return	5	similar	10	succeed	10

suddenly	4	toast		waitress	2
sugar	7	today	1	warm	5
summer	5	toe	6	wash	9
sun	6	together	8	waste	6
supermarket	7	toilet	7	watch	9
supply	5	too	6	weak	6
sure	2	tooth	6	wear	6
surprise	8	toothbrush	9	week	4
table	2	toothpaste	9	weekend	4
take	9	top	9	welcome	9
talk	1	town	4	well	1
tall	6	traffic	10	what	2
tape	6	travel	1	when	9
taste	9	tree	8	where	1
teacher	1	trip	5	white	6
telephone	3	true	4	who	1
tell	1	try	10	wide	6
tennis	7	turn	10	wife	2
text	6	TV = television	2	wind	6
thank	1	twenty	3	window	5
thanks	1	ugly	6	windy	6
there	2	umbrella	6	winter	5
these	5	uncle	8	with	7
they	4	under	4	wolf	5
thin	6	understand	7	woman	1
thing	5	underwear	6	wonderful	9
this	1	upper	7	work	2
those	5	upstairs	9	worry	4
through	9	use	6	write	1
tiger	5	vacation	5	yellow	7
till	5	vegetable	7	yesterday	8
time	2	venezuela	1	you	1
tired	1	very	1	young	6
to	4	visit	2	zero	3

Appendix B
Contractions Appearing in this Book

all's	(all is)	she's	(she is)
aren't	(are not)	that's	(that is)
doesn't	(does not)	there's	(there is)
don't	(do not)	they're	(they are)
haven't	(have not)	they've	(they have)
he's	(he is)	we're	(we are)
how'd	(how did)	what's	(what is)
I'm	(I am)	we've	(we have)
isn't	(is not)	who's	(who is)
it's	(it is)	you're	(you are)
let's	(let us)	you've	(you have)

Appendix C
Some Irregular Verbs

Infinitive	*Present*	*Progressive*
begin	begins	beginning
cost	costs	costing
cut	cuts	cutting
hear	hears	hearing
lie	lies	lying
make	makes	making
mean	means	meaning
pay	pays	paying
ring	rings	ringing
sell	sells	selling
sit	sits	sitting
stick	sticks	sticking
tell	tells	telling
take place	takes place	taking place
think about	thinks about	thinking about

*With the PRESENT CONTINUOUS, use the verb *is/are* before the *-ing* verb. Example: She is making it. - They *are* making it.

Appendix D
Some Regular Adjectives and Adverbs

Adjective	*Adverb*	*Adjective*	*Adverb*
quick	quickly	bad	badly
slow	slowly	soft	softly
glad	gladly	loud	loudly
happy	happily	early	early
careful	carefully	late	late
correct	correctly	hard	hard
nice	nicely	fast	fast
busy	busily	good	well

Appendix E
Some Irregular Comparative Forms of
Some Adjectives and Adverbs

Adjectives		*Adverbs*	
good	better	well	better
well	better		
bad	worse	badly	worse
much	more	much	more
many	more		
little	less		less
far	farther	far	farther
	further		further

Index

A

a, use of, 266, 273, 280
a/an, use of, 255, 266, 280
Adjectives, 133, 155ff. 302
    comparison, 225, 285
Adverbs, 227, 255ff.
    comparison, 227, 239,
    271, 287, 305
    too and adverb, 228
Affirmative question, 305
statement, 66
Alabama, 7
America, 44
American, 47, 48, 49, 54, 55,
    58, 68
and, use of, 172, 203
Argentina, 49, 52
around, use of, 193ff.
as...as, use of, 193, 232

B

Broadway, 288ff.
but, use of, 172

C

California, 7
Clock, the, 63, 70f.
Colors, 193ff.

Command, 125, 135, 141
Comparison, 254ff.
    adjective, 63, 255ff
Compound sentence, 181

D

Dates, 136ff.
Days of the week, 103, 113ff.
Demonstrative pronouns, 39, 125,
different, use of, 287ff.
Direct object, 244
Directions, compass, 163, 287ff.

E

England, 8
Europe, 8, 288f.
everybody, use of, 193ff.

F

Florida, 8
France, 8, 54
French, 48, 54f, 58

H

here, use of, 50
Human body, 163ff, 175

I

Idaho, 9
I'm, I'm not, use of, 54
in, use of, 193ff.
isn't, use of, 54

J

Japan, 9, 16, 18, 27, 29, 33, etc.
Japanese, 49, 51, 58, 61

L

Let's, 123

M

Mexico, 55, 170
Months, 125, 136, 138, 142f.

N

Negative statement, 66
Negatives, 39, 49, 51, 183f.
    contradictions, 39, 50f.
New York City, 164
Nobody, use of, 188
Noun object, 236f.
    Count nouns, 267
    Mass nouns, 267

Numbers from 0 to 20, 63ff.,
    80, 273
    from 2 to 100, 135
    ordinal, 93ff.

O

Object, direct/indirect, 227
    Pronoun, 125, 227, 237
on, use of, 193
one/many, use of, 104
or, use of, 173

P

Penmanship, 3
Physical description, 175
Place, review, 287
Plural, 93
Polite request, 132
Position, 255
Positive, 183
Possessive, 69
    Adjective, 63, 74
    Pronouns, 93, 99, 102, 237
    Prepositions, 93, 102, 113
Present continuous, 70, 77, 83
Pronouns, 49, 236
    Object, 136, 236, 244
    Personal, 49, 51
    Possessive, 106
    Subject, 39, 49

Q

Questions, 39, 50, 255

S

San Diego, CA, 126
Seasons, 125, 127, 134f.
Sentence, compound, 163ff.
shall, use of, 132
singular, 93
some, use of, 273, 280
Sounds, 16
Special expressions, 269
Spelling, 15
Syllabification, 16

T

Tag question, use of, 133
Telling time, 72f.
Texas, 12
This/that/there, 50
Time expressions, 63, 73, 75, 78

too, use of, 193, 240
turn off and *on*, 287

U

U.S.A., 27, 52, 55

V

Venezuela, 16, 18, 27, 48, etc.

W

Weathcr, 163ff.
wh questions, review, 219, 255
where, use of, 129, 133
with, use of, 193
who/what, use of,128
who's, use of,59
why, use of, 129
would, use of, 132
Writing, 17